study daily

THE NEW TESTAMENT

ZACHARY COWAN

ISBN: 1537455958
ISBN-13: 978-1537455952

ACKNOWLEDGMENTS

I would like to thank my wife Katie for her support, artistic development, and incredible discernment. I am thankful for Mary Einfeldt for boosting my confidence and the readability of the text with her delightful editing. Thanks to Launa Albrecht for making the cover design, so that the book might be judged without trouble of being read.

Table of Contents

Introduction. 1

Books of the New Testament

Matthew. 3

Mark. 18

Luke. 28

John. 45

Acts. 57

Romans. 72

1 Corinthians. 79

2 Corinthians. 87

Galatians. 92

Ephesians. 94

Philippians. 96

Colossians. 98

1 Thessalonians. 100

2 Thessalonians. 101

1 Timothy. 102

2 Timothy. 104

Titus. 105

Philemon. 106

Hebrews. 106

James. 111

1 Peter. 113

2 Peter. 114

1 John. 115

2 John. 117

3 John. 118

Jude. 118

Revelation. 119

Bibliography. 130

Introduction

In his landmark talk entitled, "To Sweep the Earth as with a Flood" (2014) Elder David A. Bednar shared several examples of how Latter-day Saints could use modern technologies to enhance the spread of the gospel message. Elder Bednar encouraged members to share goodness. I have never been a big user of social media, so I found this invitation difficult to apply. I thought of using the seminary's Facebook page more, but didn't feel that this would be accomplishing any kind of personal commitment. In his talk, he shared several examples of people who effectively used technology to share goodness. One of these examples was *Book of Mormon 365*, which posted a daily reading section from the Book of Mormon for one year. In addition to the reading section they also included a discussion question. My wife had been following this group for some time and really enjoyed it. When 2015 rolled around she decided to start studying the New Testament, matching current Sunday School lessons. On the first day of the year she was disappointed that the post didn't come out until around noon. She spoke about how much she enjoyed reading in the morning when she first woke up. She suggested that I could start making questions and we could develop our own study group for our families, friends, and neighbors. Later that day we created an Instagram account called *Study Daily* and told our friends and families what we were doing. I create the reading block and questions, and my wife provides the lovely photos that accompany my questions. Her pictures perfectly capture the spirit of our posts.

2014 was a particularly hard year for me and my wife. Some close friends of ours chose to leave the church. The decision to share *Study Daily* with our loved ones was motivated in part by the pain of seeing such close friends drift away. We hoped that by inviting people to study with us daily it would create an added level of protection to those that we love most. In Joseph Smith-Matthew we are told: "And whoso treasureth up my word, shall not be deceived" (1:37). I believe that scripture and wanted to make sure that my family, friends, and neighbors were being taken care of. This daily reading has allowed members to feel comfortable asking questions about parts of the scriptures that they didn't understand. It has put us on the same page literally and been a great blessing in helping them better identify, understand, feel the truth of, and apply doctrines and principles of the gospel.

In the concluding moments of his talk, Elder Bednar gave this promise to those listening, "that you may have eyes to see clearly both the possibilities and the pitfalls of the remarkable technologies that are available to us today, that you may increase in your capacity to use these inspired tools appropriately, and that you may receive inspiration and guidance about the role you should play in helping to sweep the earth as with a flood of truth and righteousness." As in countless other moments of my life I have found the words of a prophet of God to be true. This has blessed my life and the lives of others. Though these questions direct us to the scriptures and the words of prophets, I am solely responsible for the content, and do not represent the Church of Jesus Christ of Latter-days Saints.

I look forward to studying the New Testament with you and invite you to be a diligent learner. Please mark and write all over this book. The New Testament was broken up into sections that are designed to take a year to complete. You are more than welcome to study at any pace you want. Many of the questions are designed to direct your attention to find several ideas and principles with each read. I have found it to be a very rewarding practice to never study without also writing down the thoughts and feelings that I experience. If you learn anything from this book or its questions, I truly feel that it will be your own fault. The Holy Ghost is incredible at his job as teacher of the gospel. As you pray for heavenly assistance throughout your study, I promise you it will come.

Day 1, Matthew 1

As you read this chapter, consider all of the different people that God trusted with his Son. What are some of the things that God has entrusted you with?

Also look for all of the different ways that this chapter teaches us that Jesus Christ is the Son of God.

I love that Emmanuel means "God with us." As you read about people that God was with, think about times or ways that Jesus Christ has been with you (:23).

Day 2, Matthew 2

Everyone in this chapter receives messages and messengers. What can we learn from how each person or group responded to the different messages and messengers?

What can this chapter teach us about parenting and family?

Every person or group mentioned in this chapter can teach us at least one incredible truth. As you encounter each person or group, write down what lesson we can learn from them.

Day 3, Matthew 3

In Matthew 11:7-11, Jesus said that John the Baptist was a prophet and more. What impresses you about John the Baptist as you read Matthew 3?

Jesus traveled 80-90 miles to be baptized by John, and the people who went to hear John had to travel into the wilderness (:1, 5). What efforts have helped you to come closer to spiritual things?

What does Jesus' baptism teach us about obedience to God's commandments?

Day 4, Matthew 4

What can we learn about resisting temptation from Jesus' example in this chapter?

How do the stories in this chapter build your faith, or love for Jesus Christ?

In verses 18-23, Jesus called his disciples to follow him. They had several reasons not to follow him, but they chose to. How has your life been blessed by trying to follow Jesus Christ?

In verses 23-24, notice the word "all". In what ways has Jesus healed you?

Day 5, Matthew 5:1-26

For the next few days we will be studying the Sermon on the Mount, the greatest sermon/talk that has ever been given. In these verses that you read today think about what inspires you to do well.

In verse 1, Jesus left the multitude and went up a mountain. His disciples then followed. This whole chapter is an invitation to raise our thoughts, feelings, and actions. Just as a mountain is climbed one step at a time, we will start to act more like Christ one day at a time. What did you read that increased your desire to think, feel, or act more like Jesus Christ today?

Verses 2-11 are called the Beatitudes, which means "to be blessed" (see 3a). Which of these beatitudes has blessed your life?

Day 6, Matthew 5:27-48

What examples have you seen lately of people trying to live one of these teachings?

For years I've had a note in my scriptures by verses 43-47 which says in bold red letters: "This is a HARD commandment." In your life, what have your learned about how to love and care about those you don't like and may even hate?

4

The commandment to be perfect in Matthew 5:48 can be overwhelming if we forget that the Greek word for "perfect" actually means "complete, finished, [or] fully developed" (5:48b). Instead of focusing on all the things that you didn't do today to be more like Christ, I invite you to consider all the things that you did that he would be pleased with.

Day 7, Matthew 6:1-18

In Matthew 5, the Lord taught us several things that help us think, feel, and act like Him. As you study Matthew 6 you will see Jesus warns us of things that will prevent us from thinking, feeling, and acting like Him. What warnings did you find in today's section?

What did Jesus teach to improve our charity/alms giving, our prayers, or our fasting?

In these verses, Jesus warns us of hierocracy. What is wrong with doing the right thing so that others know we are doing the right thing?

Day 8, Matthew 6:19-34

What does the Lord teach about priorities and goals in this section?

What difference does it make when you try to put the things of God first rather than second?

In verses 25-34, Jesus Christ is not telling us not to plan for the future. So what *is* He teaching?

Day 9, Matthew 7

In Matthew 5, the Savior taught us many things that would help us to think, feel, and act more like Him. In Matthew 6, He warned us about hypocrisy, doing the right thing for the wrong reason. In this chapter, Jesus will warn us about the danger of judging and misjudging. Look for what you can learn about that theme in each of these sections: 1-5, 6, 7-11, 12, 13-14, 15-20, and 21-27.

Years ago I heard Brent Esplin say of verses 15-20 that "we are not to judge others, but we are expected to be fruit inspectors." What do you think is the subtle difference that the Savior is teaching between those two options?

After reading verses 21-27, how would you finish each of these?

Learning + Doing = _____.

Learning + Not Doing = _____.

In verses 28-29, the scribes had a great understanding of the scriptures. What do you think it means to teach with authority?

Day 10, Matthew 8:1-17

In this section of scripture, there are 3 great stories of healing and many incredible insights and feelings that you can learn from them. As you read look for and ponder these questions: Who was healed? How were they healed? What were they healed of? What can I learn from that?

Which of these healing stories do you like the best?

Leprosy was a pretty big deal back in the day. If you received it you became a physical wreck and a social outcast. Palsy, which was a form of paralysis, could be painful and debilitating. Leprosy and palsy are two life-changing healings, but Peter's mother-in-law simply had a "fever" (:14) and Jesus healed it. As you read this section today, ponder on how Jesus heals both major and minor afflictions. He heals the socially unclean by doing the one thing you are not supposed to do with them, touch them. He also allows the faith of those who are not afflicted, and even consider themselves unworthy, to be sufficient to bring down blessings in the "selfsame hour." What are you going to do to call upon the power of Christ's Atonement today?

Day 11, Matthew 8:18-34

Verse 24 is a great metaphor for life. When great storms come upon us, the kind that cover us with waves and it appears that Jesus is asleep and unconcerned with our condition, we would do well to keep our faith and remember that Jesus will awake and bring "a great calm" to our personal storms. When was a time you felt "a great calm" after a "great tempest"?

Which miracle have you experienced more in your life: Jesus' ability to bring "great calm" to physical or natural tempests, or His ability to cast out of ourselves and others spiritual torments?

As you read this section, you will notice that Jesus didn't always make it easy for people to follow him. Elder Holland calls Jesus "the inconvenient Messiah" (BYU Speeches, 27 February 1982). As you follow Christ He will lead you into great storms, rejection, and lack of physical rest; but if devils, winds, and waves obey Him, so can you.

Day 12, Matthew 9:1-17

In this section, Jesus performs a miracle just so others know He has power to forgive sin. This becomes a strong testimony that Jesus is a the Son of God and has the ability to forgive our sins. Every miracle from this point forward becomes an additional witness that our sins can be forgiven. Why is this so important for us to know?

In verses 10-12, there is a brief teaching that the Savior then invites us, in verse 13, to "go ye and learn what that meaneth." You may want to read verse 13 a couple of times. The Lord is not teaching us about His mercy, He is teaching that He would rather have a people who feel mercy than a people who just make sacrifice/religious offerings.

What do verses 14-15 teach about fasting?

What do you think Jesus is trying to teach in verses 14-17?

Day 13, Matthew 9:18-38

In today's section of scripture you will see several people with different problems approach the Savior, having faith that He can help them. Today, I invite you to take your problems in faith to the Savior.

Verse 20 mentions that this woman had her issue for 12 years. How do you think she kept her faith through all that time?

Why do you think people sometimes laugh and scorn those with faith? (:24)

One of our questions will be the Savior's. When facing a challenge and you have prayed for help: "Believe ye that I am able to do this?" (:28)

Day 14, Matthew 10:1-20

Matthew 9:36-38 ends with Jesus Christ recognizing the great amount of suffering and he pleads with his Father for more helpers. Matthew 10 begins with the calling of the Twelve to help fulfil Jesus' prayer. Today you will see people suffering around you, and you can do something, even if it's only a little thing, to help. Will you do it? Will you help be an answer to Jesus Christ's prayer today?

What do you think it means to be "as wise as serpents, and harmless as doves" (:16)? Why do you think we should be a combination of these two things?

When you hear the phrase "the kingdom of heaven is at hand," (:7) do you think it means that the Second Coming is close, or that we now have the teachings that are able to make our lives like the kingdom of heaven?

Day 15, Matthew 10:21-42

Yesterday Jesus called the Twelve Apostles and gave them counsel. Today that counsel continues and may seem a little odd, but if each idea is looked at through a question, a theme emerges. Which way do you face?

There are some great phrases and ideas that are repeated so we don't miss them. In verses 26-31 look for what we are to fear, and what we are not to fear.

Pay attention to the phrase, "A cold cup of water" (:42). No effort to serve others is ever wasted, not even the smallest of gestures. What small acts of service will you give or receive today?

Day 16, Matthew 11

What evidence does Jesus provide in this chapter that He is the Christ, the promised Messiah?

There have always been reasons not to believe in prophets and in Jesus Christ. There have also been reasons *to* believe. If there is music it is your choice to dance, or not (:16). The choice not to dance does not mean that there is no music, and there is music in this thing called Christ.

Verses 28-30 are some of the most well-known of all time. What have you learned from these verses? What have you felt because of these verses? What experiences have you had because of these verses?

Day 17, Matthew 12:1-23

The Pharisees were obsessed with the "dos" and "don'ts" of Sabbath day observance. Notice that Jesus was more concerned about the Sabbath making us a merciful people and providing a chance for Him to heal others. He was less concerned with the sacrifice of animals, time, and activities. How are your Sabbath days? Are you using the Sabbath day to heal soul, family, friends, and others, or are you just doing not doing things?

I love the prophetic description of Jesus in verse 20, He will not break a bruised reed, or put out a smoking flax. So long as you have strength to stand, and even a smoldering ember of faith He will not give up on you. Why do you think this is important for us to know?

Day 18, Matthew 12:24-50

When people accuse us of being evil or doing evil things, what does the Savior teach us about how to respond to them, and how to know good from evil?

What do verses 34-37 teach about speech?

In verses 38-42, they asked for a sign. An adulterous generation seeks after signs. This may appear a little confusing at first. Just as an adulterer seeks for personal pleasure before commitment, so a sign seeker wants proof before committing to believe. They will get no sign but the sign of Jonah.

Verses 43-45 teaches us that it is not enough to remove bad influences from our lives, we must replace them with something good, or those evil habits are likely to return stronger.

Day 19, Matthew 13:1-30

What changes need to happen to the unproductive soil/hearts so that growth and healing are possible?

Rather than looking at what kind of soil you have been over your whole life, consider your soil quality of the last week. What about last sacrament meeting, or Sunday school lesson? If you approach each spiritual opportunity trying to be good ground you will have tremendous growth.

From time to time people question God about His decision to allow evil to occur in this world. What does the parable of the wheat and the tares in verses 24-30 teach us about why God allows evil to happen?

Day 20, Matthew 13:31-58

Jesus gives an interpretation for some of the parables that He shares, but He offers nothing for the parables in verses 31-32, 33, and 52. What do you think we can learn about the kingdom of heaven from these parables?

Verses 54-58 is one of the best places in all of scripture to learn about the half brothers and sisters of Jesus. We also learn why Jesus couldn't or wouldn't perform miracles in his own town.

Day 21, Matthew 14:1-21

Which of these do you think hurt Herod more: his uncontrolled lust, or his inability to withstand peer pressure?

What is the difference between trying to please yourself, trying to please others, and trying to please God?

All of us have had, and will have, bad days. The day that Jesus was informed of the death of His cousin John must have been a bad day (:12). He sought the opportunity to be alone, yet the multitude followed (:13). He could have turned them away; instead He taught us one of the best ways to overcome bad days is by serving others. The next time you have a bad day, will you follow the example of Jesus by serving and having compassion for others?

Day 22, Matthew 14:22-36

Jesus frequently took time for personal prayer and worship (:23). Why is personal worship important in your life?

Faith and fear are two elements in today's story about Jesus and Peter walking on water. What can we learn about faith and fear that will help us?

Day 23, Matthew 15:1-21

Many make the mistake of defending or teaching tradition and policy rather than doctrine and commandment. Notice how Jesus continually teaches that commandments are greater than tradition.

Which of these is most likely to defile you today: gossip, profanity, or angry words (:11)?

I love to imagine verse 14. Take a minute to visualize it yourself. Who is leading you, and how well do they see?

Draught in Greek means a stinky toilet. That's right, Jesus is going to use potty language to teach us. What do you think He is teaching in verses 15-20?

Day 24, Matthew 15:21-39

Jesus' ministry was only to the House of Israel, or to members of the covenant. He is not trying to be mean to this Canaanite woman, but no parent would feed the family pet and not the children. Realizing that she had not made a covenant to receive these blessings, she still asks for mercy, and He rewards her faith. Many, despite whatever church they attend are blessed and healed because of faith in Jesus (:21-28).

When our problems and issues drive us to the feet of Jesus (:30), we are acknowledging that we can't fix it and that He can. That is humble faith. What problem or issue will you cast at His feet today? Notice that in verse 30 it was other people's problems that the multitude cast at His feet.

If we are willing to give the Savior our time, talents, and possessions, however little they may be, He will multiply them to bless us and others. When have you experienced this (:32-39)?

Day 25, Matthew 16

In verses 1-12, Jesus warns His Apostles and us about the corrupting doctrine of the Pharisees and the Sadducees. Jesus has performed several miracles so far, yet they continue to ask for more signs, more proof. The corrupting doctrine is that belief comes from proof/signs. They are still asking for signs because miracles don't produce faith. A correct example of how to obtain belief follows when Peter explains why he believes Jesus is the Christ in verses (:13-17). Is your belief in Christ based on proof, signs, wonders, miracles, or revelation from Heavenly Father?

How has the promise in verses 18-19 blessed your life?

What additional insights can you learn from the footnotes 18a, 24d, and 25a?

Day 26, Matthew 17

What can we learn about how to treat spiritual experiences from verses 1-13?

As you read verses 14-21, look for why Jesus was able to heal this boy when some of His disciples couldn't?

Verses 24-27 contain my favorite tax collection story. What did you learn from it?

Day 27, Matthew 18:1-20

What does Jesus teach us about how to move toward heaven and how to avoid hell in verses 1-10?

Why do you think it is important for us to know how God feels about those who repent (:11-13)?

What do verses 19-20 teach us about why we gather together to worship?

Day 28, Matthew 18:21-35

What lesson or lessons do you think Peter learned from Christ's story?

There are several characters in this story. Which role will you play this week?

True or false, God's forgiveness of our sins is dependent upon our forgiveness of others.

Day 29, Matthew 19

What can we learn from how Jesus defended the importance of marriage and family in verses 1-15?

If you were to ask the question "What lack I yet" (:20). How do you think the Lord would answer you?

Two key components to discipleship are following and forsaking. Which of those do you need more right now in your quest for discipleship (:16-30)?

Day 30, Matthew 20:1-16

What does the parable of laborers teach you about God's kindness, mercy, understanding, and desire to bless all of his children?

What does this parable teach about how ungrateful, entitled, judgmental, and complaining we can be?

Sometimes we focus so much on the reward/penny that we forget what a great blessing it is to labor all our days in the Lord's vineyard. How has laboring for the Lord blessed your life?

Day 31, Matthew 20:17-34

Verses 17-19 are a great summary of Matthew chapters 21-28.

What does Jesus say about who will be in heaven (:20-28)?

I adore the story found in verses 29-34. What insights can you learn by looking closely are the following words and phrases: "multitude," "followed him," "have mercy on us," "cried the more," "stood still," and "compassion"?

Day 32, Matthew 21:1-22

This whole chapter is a testimony of Jesus' divinity. Throughout the book of Matthew Jesus has been telling people to keep quiet about who He is and the miracles that He has performed. Where in these verses do you see examples of Jesus coming out in open acknowledgment that He is the Messiah?

Symbolically an ass represents humility, peace, unyielding, and work. A horse represents war, military, and strength. Which one of these do you figuratively ride around your town and house?

The fig tree looked the part of a productive fruit producer, but it only had the appearance. It had put on airs/leaves without any fruit. The tree was a type of hypocrite and a reminder that there can't be two different versions of us.

Day 33, Matthew 21:23-46

In today's section Jesus will tie himself to the prophets. Whatever you can say about one of these authority you can say about the other (:23-27). Your belief and repentance in one will lead to your belief and repentance in the other (:28-32). How you treat one will determine how you will treat the other (:33-41). How is your relationship with Jesus and His prophets? How do we respond when they come to check on the fruitfulness of our rented vineyards?

Jesus and His teachings will be a nuisance, unless we build on them. Is there a teaching of Jesus that you are tripping on that would bless your life more by building on it (:42-44)?

What can we learn from the additional footnotes :32d, 33a, and 45a?

Day 34, Matthew 22:1-22

Verses 1-14 are called "the parable of the marriage of the king's son." Here are some additional names that it could be called: "The parable of the invited guests," "The parable of the guests who refused to attend," "The parable of the wedding garment". After reading the parable, which name do you think best describes the principles that you learned, or do you have a name to offer?

What phrases in verses 3-6 do you think are great mini lessons?

Money is usually printed in the image of political leaders. Read Genesis 1:26-27 to see what image we are minted in. Christ is teaching us that we are both citizens and disciples (:15-22).

Day 35, Matthew 22:23-46

It might be helpful to read about the Sadducees and Pharisees in your Bible Dictionary. What did you learn about each group?

Verses 23-33 sound contradictory to Jesus' teaching in Matthew 19:6 about marriage. The key is in the context. The question to Jesus was posed by the Sadducees, who do not believe in immortality or the resurrection (:23). Jesus teaches what the scriptures say about those who are married without the resurrection in mind (see :30c). Then Jesus focuses on the immortality of Abraham, Isaac, and Jacob (:32). That is the astonishing doctrine that Jesus taught in verse 33, that you, your neighbor, and each of us are eternal beings. How does this doctrine make your life a little more astonishing?

See what difference it will make in your life today to do the same things that you always do, but with the thought that you are doing these things because you love God and love others.

For one month we have studied the words and teachings of Jesus Christ. So, "what think ye of Christ?" (:42)

Day 36, Matthew 23:1-22

You may want to read about scribes in your Bible Dictionary today.

"Woe unto you, scribes and Pharisees, hypocrites," "blind guides," "fools", "blind." Over the next two days you will see these words and phrases repeated a lot. Why do you think doing things to be seen by others (:5) is so dangerous that Jesus pronounces several woes for doing such?

Verses 11-12 are the solution to hypocrisy, but they are hard, very hard.

Day 37, Matthew 23:23-39

Day two of "Woe unto you, scribes and Pharisees, hypocrites," "blind guides," "fools," "blind." Why do you think the Savior calls them "fools" and "blind?" How do you think they are being fools, and what are they blind to?

Hypocrisy is so dangerous that in verse 33 that the Savior asked the question "how can ye escape the damnation of hell?" His answer is verses 34-39. What did you discover?

What difference does it make if we change the word "house" to household in verse 38?

Day 38, Matthew 24:1-28

Joseph Smith-Matthew is found in the Pearl of Great Price and is the inspired translation of Matthew chapter 24.

Verses 1-22 deal with the prophesied destruction of the temple and Jerusalem, which happened in 70 A.D. Verses 23-51 are signs of the Second Coming.

The language in verse 12 haunts me. What are you doing to keep your love for God, self, and others warm?

Where is your holy place? What difference do holy places make in your life? Do you think a holy place is more about where, or how we live (:15)?

Day 39, Matthew 24:29-51

Which do you think is more important, knowing and tracking all of the signs of the Second Coming, or preparing to present ourselves to the Savior?

Verse 34 has reference to both the generation of Christ who would see the destruction of the temple, and the generation who would see a fulfillment of the Second Coming signs.

There are many books that you don't have to buy if you remember verse 36.

Day 40, Matthew 25:1-30

Yesterday you read many of the signs about the Second Coming. Today we will study two parables to help us prepare for death or Christ's return. In both parables we have a group that is expecting him, waiting for him, and yet some were not ready. That is foolish and slothful. We know that the Savior will come again. That means that we will either be wise or foolish. In the last few days what have you done to put yourself into the wise group? What have you done to put yourself into the foolish group? What have you done so that He might know you (:12)?

"Afterward" there is something to learn about timing and promptness from this, what do you think it is (:11)?

If the message of these two parables is not the same, what do you think the message of each is?

Day 41, Matthew 25:31-46

What problems happen when we try to separate left from right, goat from sheep, rather than leaving it to Jesus?

What will you do unto Christ today, by doing it unto others?

Why do you think that Jesus takes the treatment of the least, the most dull, boring, uninteresting of people so personal (:40, 45)?

Day 42, Matthew 26:1-35

What can we learn by comparing and contrasting the woman and her actions against those of Judas and the chief priests in verses 1-16?

Why do you think we eat and drink these symbolic emblems? Why do you think the bread is broken? Do you use the sacrament as an opportunity to give thanks (:27)? Why do you think Jesus asked them to "Drink ye all of it" (:27)? It is interesting that Jesus has only partaken of the sacrament once, when we do it so often. What purpose do you think singing a hymn serves (:30)?

In today's section there are several places that show Jesus' ability to know the future (:2, 17-18, 21, 29, 31-32, 33-34). Why do you think this is important for us to know?

Day 43, Matthew 26:36-75

Look for all of the places where Christ could have become upset and said or did something unkind, yet he doesn't. He controls Himself, He understands, He uses kind words. Who will you forgive, be kinder to, and have more patience with today?

Day 44, Matthew 27:1-26

What kinds of conversations, discussions, and councils do you have about others? Are they against them or for them (:1)?

What kinds of thoughts and feelings do you have about verses 3-10?

As you read verses 11-26, notice how many opportunities Pilate had to make the right choice. What opportunities to do the right thing will you now have the courage to do today?

Day 45, Matthew 27:27-50

Those who passed made their belief in Jesus conditional on what they wanted Him to do rather than on what He wanted them to do (:40-43). Our lives and choices are different are when we say "because Jesus is the Christ" rather than "If Jesus is the Christ." What will you do today because Jesus is the Christ?

What important lesson do you think we are supposed to learn from verse 46?

Let's not let curiosity or experiments keep us from kindness (:46-49).

Day 46, Matthew 27:51-66

As you read, look for additional evidence that Jesus and others were actually resurrected. I love that both believer and unbeliever prepared for Him to stay in the tomb.

The veil traditionally separated people from the Ark of the Covenant or the throne of God. When the veil ripped it was symbolic that all could return to God now that Christ had finished the Atonement. This is just another reason that the sacrament bread is ripped, broken, or parted (:51).

The centurion in verse 54 needed an earthquake to learn who Jesus was. What did you need?

How people speak and treat the dead always reveals the depth of their love and devotion (:57-60).

Day 47, Matthew 28

Notice the words "fear" and "afraid" in verses 1-10. Think about how these women overcame fear to become the first great witnesses of the resurrected Christ.

Verses 11-15 serve as additional evidence that Jesus' body didn't stay in the tomb. It is also neat that only "some of the watch" took money in exchange for what they witnessed (:11).

Verses 16-20 are packed full of meaning and significance. What word, phrase, or verse did you find a great truth in?

Day 48, Mark 1:1-22

Welcome to the Gospel of Mark, written with a gentile audience in mind and universally acknowledged by scholars as the earliest written of the gospels. One thing you will notice about Mark is how fast the book moves. The 22 verses that we will cover today is a shorter version of Matthew chapters 1-4.

Mark gives no generational genealogy of Jesus. He simply states that Jesus is the "Son of God" (:1). Mark will focus more on Jesus' actions than his words. What does Jesus do in today's section that convinces you that He is the Son of God?

Day 49, Mark 1:23-45

You will notice in Mark that nearly everything happens "immediately," "straightway," or "forthwith" (:10, 12, 18, 20, 21, 28, 31, 42). This is a way to show Jesus' power and authority.

The Savior's example to have solitary prayer in his worship is an invitation for us to do the same (:35).

Verses 43-45 are interesting because of the paradox that they create. We are to be careful with spiritual events, yet it is also good for us to publish and blaze abroad our experiences. What do you think about this former leper sharing that which he was told not to?

Day 50, Mark 2

If we pay careful attention we will notice how the events of the week and the feelings that they supply will answer the reasoning of our hearts (:6-8).

Is our social circle big enough to include those who need help and don't always make the best decisions (:15-17)?

Verse 27 is one of the best teachings about the importance of the Sabbath day. Our God is not an ego maniac. He created the Sabbath because we need the blessings that come from keeping it, not because He needs people to worship Him. How can this verse change how people view the Sabbath day?

Day 51, Mark 3:1-19

Do we watch what others do on the Sabbath so we might accuse and find fault with them (:2)?

When Jesus asks us to stretch, it results in healing and wholeness. Watch for how He will ask you to stretch today (:5).

Jesus loves to give righteous nicknames. If Jesus were to give you a righteous nickname what do you think, or want it to be (:16-17)?

Day 52, Mark 3:20-35

The unclean spirits knew who Jesus was, but His friends thought He was crazy, and the scribes thought He was evil (:11-12, 21-22).

In order for Satan to spoil our lives and our families he must bind us first. He cannot do that if we remain close to the spirit, thus his warning about blasphemy against the Holy Ghost.

Because the scribes accused Jesus of not having the Spirit (:22, 28-30). He taught them about blasphemy against the Holy Ghost. To do that, a person can't just have the Spirit and then reject it. To commit this sin, one must do what the scribes accused Jesus of becoming: a person like Satan, that is why there is no forgiveness for this sin, because there is no repentance (:28a).

Day 53, Mark 4:1-20

Congratulations on being good ground. Now, the questions are: Are you better ground now than you were a month ago when we last read this parable? Are you allowing and applying these teachings to bring forth 30, 60, or 100 fold blessings into your life?

Can you identify the things that are attempting to choke/stunt the growth/belief of the words of the scriptures, prophets, and Jesus?

Being "alone" with the scriptures, being alone to ponder, being alone to prayerfully ask questions is key to getting answers (:10). When in the last week have you felt the blessings of being alone in personal worship?

Day 54, Mark 4:21-41

Yesterday we read the parable of the sower, where the seed/word was planted in different grounds. Verses 21-25 are trying to help us determine how we treat the word.

We have two parables about the kingdom of God: verses 26-29 the parable about the seed growing secretly, and verses 30-32 the parable of the mustard seed. Which one do you like better and what does it teach you about the kingdom of God on earth?

Verses 35-41 tell an amazing story. What does this teach you about Jesus? What does this teach you about fear and faith? What does this teach you about storms and peace?

Day 55, Mark 5:1-20

Verses 1-20 give another great story. Notice how these devils treated the bodies that they took possession of: either man or swine. What does that teach you about our bodies and what does it teach you about evil spirits?

This formerly possessed man becomes a missionary that causes others to marvel because the Lord's compassion has changed his life, and put him in "his right mind" (:15-20). We have all had experiences that should similarly compel us to do missionary work.

Day 56, Mark 5:21-43

Verses 25-28 give us more information about this woman and how difficult her challenge was. Yet, she still believed she could be healed. Why is it so impressive that after all of this she kept reaching out to Jesus?

Jesus was not planning on healing Jairus' daughter, nor this woman. What does this story teach us about how to inadvertently bless the lives of others?

Why do you think it is important that Jesus asked those who were mocking and laughing to leave before He healed the little girl (:40)?

Day 57, Mark 6:1-30

In verses 1-6 look for reasons why Jesus was not able to do any mighty works in His home town?

What do you think is the most impressive thing that the Apostles are asked to do and not to do in verses 7-13?

Verses 14-29 contain the story of John the Baptist's death. Look for how Herod makes one bad choice after another. It becomes increasingly hard to choose the right when we consistently choose the wrong.

Day 58, Mark 6:31-56

Several times in the scriptures we see the Savior combining teaching and eating. How will you use feeding times as teaching times this week?

The night was divided into four watches. The first was from 6-9 p.m., the second was from 9-12 a.m., the third was from 12-3 a.m., and the fourth was from 3-6 a.m. Why do you think it is important for us to know that we worship a fourth watch God (:48)?

Elder Holland has said that to "be of good cheer" may be the most broken commandment ("The Tongues of Angels" *Ensign,* May 2007). Why do you think it is so hard to be of good cheer? How often do you struggle with keeping it?

Day 59, Mark 7:1-13

You may want to mark the word "tradition" as it comes up in your reading today.

What do verses 6-9 say about the conflict of tradition vs. commandments?

Do you have any traditions that are causing your lips to honor God, but are removing your heart from Him?

Check out the word "Corban" in your Bible Dictionary, this will help unlock verses 10-13.

Day 60, Mark 7:14-37

Yesterday Jesus dealt with the tradition of being spiritually unclean if hands and cups were not washed correctly. Now, washing your hands before a meal is a good thing, but it doesn't determine your spirituality. Today in verses 14-23, look for how Jesus teaches that what we think about and desire impacts our spirituality.

Verse 24 and footnote 24a gives us some wonderful insight into Jesus. Why can't He and we just hide away?

In verses 29-30 we see that Jesus didn't have to lay his hands on the daughter's head or touch her in order to heal her. Then we get this story of the deaf and dumb in verses 31-37 where Jesus not only touches, but does it in a very unusual way. What do you think is the purpose of touching or laying hands on someone who needs to be healed?

Day 61, Mark 8:1-21

From the ingredients of seven loaves and "a few small fishes" Jesus produces a meal that feeds 4,000 and leaves several baskets full (:7). Sometimes we feel that our talents, skills, and efforts are too little to make a difference. Jesus can take our loves/efforts and he can multiply them. When have you experienced Christ increasing your talents and efforts? What little thing will you offer today that Christ can use to help many more?

The Pharisees of Dalmanutha approached Jesus wanting a sign/miracle like the feeding of the 4,000. Yet, they had not been in the wilderness with Him for three days, nor did they bring any loaves or fish (:1-2). Jesus could/would do nothing because they provided nothing. The only thing He could do was depart (:13). How can this relate to us?

Day 62, Mark 8:22-38

What things does the story in verses 22-26 teach us about healing, recovering, and how Jesus can help us with our problems?

Because discipleship is about growth and direction, there will be times when we feel good about ourselves and times when we don't. As you read verses 27-33 consider what Peter might have been feeling at different moments. How do you think this experience might have helped Peter?

Sometimes when I am tempted to do something that I know is wrong, I think or say to myself, "Well, it's not the world." Reminding me that what I would get for doing the wrong thing is not that great of a deal (:36-38).

Day 63, Mark 9:1-29

In what ways has Jesus been transfigured or changed to become more important during your life?

Verses 21-22 give us some extra details about what life must have been like for this father-and-son team.

Jesus helps this father who has his doubts and discouragements. What do you think this story can teach us about doubt and belief that can help you?

Day 64, Mark 9:30-50

The Apostles missed out on an opportunity to learn because they were afraid to ask questions. Asking questions is an act of faith. We ask because we believe there is an answer.

Which of these scripture chunks, 9:33-37, and 9:38-41, do you find most helpful in helping you not want to be jealous of, or compare yourself to others?

In the first reading, it looks like verses 42-48 are about self-inflicted dismemberment, but footnote 43a helps us out a lot. As you read the footnote notice what each body part symbolizes.

Day 65, Mark 10:1-31

I believe that verse 1 contains the great secret of good teaching: "he taught them again." It is not enough to teach correct principles once. They must be taught again and again.

I think verses 17-31 contain several power phrases. Phrases that are taken one at a time and pondered can become sermons. Which of the following power phrases do you like the best: "one running, and kneeled to him" (:17), "Master, all these have I observed from my youth" (:20), "Then Jesus beholding him loved him" (:21), "give to the poor" (:21), "went away grieved: for he had great possessions" (:22), "the disciples were astonished" (:24, 26), "for them that trust in riches" (:24), or "With men it is impossible, but not with God: for with God all things are possible" (:27)?

Day 66, Mark 10:32-52

If you were a disciple and you heard Jesus explain verses 33-34, which feeling do you think would be more dominate, amazement or fear?

In verses 35-45, look for what James and John did not understand about leadership. What did Jesus teach them to correct their misunderstanding?

As you read verses 66-52, look for all of the reasons why Bartimaeus shouldn't have been healed, and also look for all of the reasons that he was.

Day 67, Mark 11:1-18

What does the story in verses 1-6 teach us about Jesus' awareness of the future? How can this increase our faith?

The story of Jesus' triumphant entry into Jerusalem is one of only a few stories that are in all four of the Gospels. Look up the word "hosanna" in your Bible Dictionary to get a better understanding of what they were saying.

There are not many things for people to be critical about Jesus, but in this chapter we have two stories that people sometimes have questions about. The first is the fig tree being cursed in verses 12-14 and the second is the cleansing of the temple in verses 15-18. How are these stories actually incredible teaching moments?

Day 68, Mark 11:19-33

Yesterday Jesus cursed a fig tree. The next day it had withered away. Look for what Jesus teaches about faith, belief, doubt, and desire in verses 19-24.

What do you think that our forgiveness is conditional upon in verses 25-26?

When it comes to religion, it is either of God or of man and we will get no answers until we are willing to decide (:27-33). What is your answer? Is this all of heaven or of man?

Day 69, Mark 12:1-27

In verses 1-12 notice how many people were "sent" to the husbandmen. What does that teach you about God's desire and determination to save His people?

What does verse 19 teach you about how important family and children were to these people?

The Lord associated erring or making mistakes with not reading and knowing the scriptures in verses 24-27. In what ways has scripture study helped you avoid errors?

For more understanding upon Jesus' teachings regarding marriage, see day 35.

Day 70, Mark 12:28-44

Which of the two great commandments mentioned in verses 30-31 do you personally find more challenging? How about your family? How about your community? How about our nation?

Jesus told the scribe who began to see the importance of loving God and neighbor that he was "not far from the kingdom of God" (:34). How are you going to collapse the distance between heaven and yourself today by loving God and others better?

What does the Savior teach us about worship from the examples of the scribes and the widow in verses 38-41?

Day 71, Mark 13:1-20

There are two entrees in the Bible Dictionary that can help us to better understand the history behind Jesus' prophecy in verses 1-20 about Jerusalem's destruction in 70 A.D. by the Romans. The first is "Temple, of Herod" and the second is the "Abomination of Desolation".

Notice when things are at their worst, Jesus teaches us to continue to pray for things that will make it easier, and Jesus promises for the elect's sake that the days will be shortened (:15). If you are in the middle of really hard days, hold on. The Lord has promised that they will be shortened for your sake.

Day 72, Mark 13:21-37

To be elect does not mean better. It means elected to have the gospel and to help others receive it. Read verses 20-27 and see what Christ teaches those who are elected.

In verses 32-37 we are told several times to "watch." Here are a couple of helpful cross-references: 36a, and Mosiah 4:30.

Servants are given authority over each other, but in order to use that authority correctly they must do what their master would do. What does that teach us about church callings (:34)?

Day 73, Mark 14:1-26

Why do you think it reads "she hath done what she could" rather than she hath done what she *should* (:8)? How is Jesus' wording in this verse a good formula for how we should take care of others?

The phrase "conveniently betray him" in verse 11 is interesting to me. Jesus and His gospel are seldom convenient. It is the inconvenience of Jesus that really changes us in the end. How will your life be inconvenienced and bettered today because of your belief in Jesus?

It is a more difficult thing to say "is it I?" (:19) rather than "is it her, him, or them?" Examining our own lives when we hear talks and lessons will benefit us much more than looking for how they apply to others. How could this idea of "is it I?" bless your life?

Day 74, Mark 14:27-53

In verses 27-31 look for how the word "all" is used. Peter struggled to understand that the Savior knew that "this day" and "this night" everyone would deny Him, run from Him, be offended by Him, and not be perfect (:30). We would all respond like the Apostles declaring our firmness and commitment to even die with Him. Yet, Jesus came because we all at some point turn from, run from, and even deny Him.

What insight does footnote 33a give us into what Jesus experienced?

Elder Holland taught that Abba means "daddy" or from the lips of a smaller child "papa" ("The Hands of the Fathers" *Ensign,* May. 1999). How does this change how you think about this prayer?

Verses 50-52 add a wonderful little detail to the garden scene.

Day 75, Mark 14:54-72

What can verses 54-64 teach us about witnessing/testifying?

It is dreadfully ironic what these servants do to Jesus, but He is majestic in living his cheek-turning doctrine. How can you respond better to the small injustices that you will face today?

One of the most helpful and difficult things in life, is to have old sins and mistakes "called to mind" (:72). This recollection usually produces in us the same result as it did in Peter, we tearfully repent. Reflect upon a time when the Holy Ghost helped you to repent by calling to your mind former sins and mistakes.

Day 76, Mark 15:1-25

Jesus is called the "King of the Jews" several times in this chapter see verses 2, 9, 12, 18, and 26. The title was bestowed, but not allegiance. In what ways has Jesus been the King of you this week?

What is the difference between how Jesus and Pilate handled the crowds and questions?

Notice how this large and loud group got what they wanted. What do you think we should learn from this section of verses about how to respond when the numbers and noise call on us to do what we know is wrong (:6-15)?

How often do we, like this foolish crowd, choose something else over Jesus and His teachings? How do you think this made, and makes Jesus feel?

Day 77, Mark 15:26-47

Those who mocked, railed, and wagged their heads at Jesus didn't understand. They thought that Jesus couldn't save Himself. What they didn't understand was that He *wouldn't* save Himself so that He could save us. They misunderstood that Jesus' love for God and us was greater than his love for Himself. Do you understand how good Jesus really is at living the commandments to love God and His neighbor?

Why do you think we often try to declare the terms and conditions of our belief (:32)?

I had a thought as I read verses 37-47. There have been more mortal people who have seen the resurrected Christ than those who witnessed him die. Why do you think it is important to have both witnesses of his death and of his resurrection?

Day 78, Mark 16:1-20

Look for all of the people who tell and are told about Jesus in this chapter. Telling others about our experiences with Jesus is important. Who will you tell about Jesus this week? Remember, "Be not affrighted" (:6).

Look for what you can discover about unbelief and belief in verses 11-18. Which belief would you rather have, the belief to perform signs and wonders, or the belief that does not require signs and wonders?

I love the phrase "the Lord working with them" (:20). When have you felt the truthfulness of that statement in your own personal ministry?

Day 79, Luke 1:1-20

Read verses 1-4 and 1a, looking for all of the reasons that Luke writes his account of Jesus' life.

What can the experience of Zacharias and Elisabeth teach us about receiving answers to prayers?

Do you think there is a connection in verse 15 between what we drink and what we feel (see also Daniel 1-2, D&C 89:18-21)?

What can you learn about Elias from the Bible Dictionary?

Day 80, Luke 1:21-38

As you read verses 21-38 look for how God and His angels feel about women and motherhood.

1:30 How is your favor with God? God entrusted Mary to be the mother of His Only Begotten Son. What has he entrusted you with?

When it comes to the conception of Jesus we don't know more than what is said in verse 35.

In what ways can verse 37 be powerful and life altering?

Day 81, Luke 1:39-56

My friend Taylor likes to watch the Bible videos for each scripture block. Check out this sweet clip of today's reading by searching the internet for LDS Bible video Mary and Elisabeth.

As you read or watch, look for testimony, both who shares it and what they testify of. Which testimony did you personally find the most inspiring?

Day 82, Luke 1:57-80

Noticing how the Lord shows great mercy in the lives of others increases our ability to rejoice (:58). Who do you know that has received a tender mercy from the Lord? How can you rejoice for them and with them?

When Zacharias' mouth is opened he makes an incredible prophecy that the people "noised abroad" and "laid them up in their hearts" (:65-66). Carefully read this prophecy in verses 67-80 and look for what phrases you would lay up in your heart.

Day 83, Luke 2:1-20

These may be the best known verses in the whole Bible. As you read them you will have music, movies, and family traditions come to your mind followed by feelings in your heart. What is your favorite part of these verses and why?

How does footnote 7b change our understanding about how that day must have gone?

29

Why do you think God sent shepherds, fishermen, and us to tell people about Jesus? Why not just keep sending angels?

Day 84, Luke 2:21-52

As you read verses 21-39 pay careful attention to what Simeon and Anna did so that they were prepared for the special experience of meeting their Savior.

Why do you think Luke picked the story in verses 40-52 to tell about Jesus as a child? I'm sure the Apostles knew others, so what does this story teach that makes it worth sharing and recording?

What do verses 40 and 52 say about the rest of Jesus' childhood?

Day 85, Luke 3:1-38

John tells the people that they should bring forth fruits worthy of repentance (:8). What acts does John ask us to correct in verses 7-14?

Many people thought and believed that John was the Messiah because of his miraculous birth and tragic death. Look for what John says to persuade them that he is not the Messiah?

Verses 22-38 seems like an odd place for a genealogy to show up, unless you look at the first couple of verses and the last. What do you think Luke was trying to teach by inserting this?

Day 86, Luke 4:1-30

Look at verses 1-13. Elder David O. McKay, then a member of the Quorum of the Twelve Apostles, said, "Nearly every temptation that comes to you and me comes in one of those forms. Classify them, and you will find that under one of those three nearly every given temptation that makes you and me spotted, ever so little maybe, comes to us as (1) a temptation of the appetite; (2) a yielding to the pride and fashion and vanity of those alienated from the things of God; or (3) a gratifying of the passion, or a desire for the riches of the world, or power among men" (Conference Report, Oct. 1911, 59). Which of these do you think Satan has had the most success with?

In verses 14-19 Jesus gets up and reads a scripture that everyone knows is about the promised Messiah. Then, in verses 20-27 Jesus tells the people that He is the fulfillment of this scripture and gives two examples of other prophets who were rejected. In verses 28-30 the people are angry and they attempt to kill Jesus, who escapes miraculously as He passes through the crowd. As you read these verses look for what Jesus testifies about himself and what he will do. Also look for the reasons that Christ's own testimony about himself being the Messiah was rejected.

Day 87, Luke 4:31-44

How would you finish this statement: "The devils in this section teach us that knowing Jesus is the Christ is less important than . . ."

Why do you think it is interesting that the healings in verses 38-40 happen because of the efforts of others?

What can we learn from the fact that Jesus doesn't stay with those who believe in Him, surely life would have been more comfortable if He stayed?

Day 88, Luke 5:1-16

When have you experienced tremendous blessings in your life because you were willing to do what the Savior asked you to?

Lepers would have become social outcasts because of their disease. The rule was firm, don't touch them, yet Jesus touches this man (:12-13). What are we supposed to learn from Christ's example here?

Are there limits to how many Christ can heal?

How has private prayer and worship rejuvenated your spirit this week?

Day 89, Luke 5:17-39

Which of the following do you find the most intriguing: the tremendous effort by the palsy man's friends, the forgiving of the sins, or the physical healing (:17-26)?

What strange or miraculous things have you seen today?

What do you think Jesus is trying to teach the Scribes and Pharisees who, like old leather wineskins, had become hard and inflexible (:37a), and thus could not withstand the fermentation process of new wine (:36-39)?

Day 90, Luke 6:1-26

When it came to the Sabbath day, the Pharisees were more concerned with being right than getting it right. There would be more healing, more mercy, and more understanding if we focused more on getting it right, rather than being right.

Jesus prayed all night over choosing the Twelve Apostles. What are the things and who are the people that you are currently praying over?

Which one have you seen more in your life: the blessings of verses 20-23, or the woe and warning of verses 24-26?

Day 91, Luke 6:27-49

Why do you think the gospel of Jesus Christ is so concerned with how we treat people who are different than us?

Why is verse 38 a good way to describe the blessings we receive for living the gospel?

The Lord has asked us not to judge the final condition of people, but he expects us to make good choices. Look for what choices the Lord expects us to make in verses 39-49.

Day 92, Luke 7:1-30

The centurion in this chapter did not require Jesus to come into his house, because he didn't feel worthy. However, he knew that Jesus' power was so incredible that the sick servant could be healed with just a word. Because of this, Jesus proclaimed that the man had great faith. How is your faith? Do you have to see Jesus, or have Him enter your home before you allow Him to heal you? Or, without seeing Him, does He work miracles in your life?

President Monson has shared the story from verses 10-17 several times in General Conference. He once explained that these verses are the source for how and why he learned to care for the widows in his ward as a young bishop ("A Provident Plan-A Precious Promise" *Ensign,* April 1986, 62).

The Lord only expects us to share what we have seen, heard, and know (:22). Does that make missionary work easier or harder for you?

Day 93, Luke 7:31-50

In verses 31-35 look for what the attitude of fault-finding caused this group of people to miss.

In what ways does fault-finding cause us to love and believe less?

Which of the two individuals in verses 36-50 are you most like? Do you invite the Lord into your life to question the validity of His statements, actions, and desires or do you seek him out, even if inconvenient, to receive a remission of your sins?

Day 94, Luke 8:1-25

Look up "parables" in the Bible Dictionary. It is a little long, but has some incredible insight.

What type of ground are you typically during the sacrament, other lessons, and your scripture study? What type of ground will you be next time (:11-15)?

What can the story in verses 22-25 teach us about solving stressful problems?

Day 95, Luke 8:26-56

What was this man's quality of life like before and after meeting Jesus? Which change do you think is more impressive: the big and immediate ways that Jesus changes lives or the long slow almost imperceptible changes that take years?

Why do you think that believing in and waiting for Jesus so often go together (:40)?

This is the third time we have studied this story (:41-56). This time read it slowly, carefully, and maybe even out loud. What new detail, thought, or feeling did you notice?

Day 96, Luke 9:1-17

What connection do you think there is between preaching, teaching, and healing? They are often mentioned together in the scriptures.

Why is rendering an account of what we have done and important principle of leadership?

The disciples only had five loaves and two fishes. How would you finish this phrase? "When we are willing to give all that we have to the Lord, then he can..." (:11-17).

Day 97, Luke 9:18-36

Is there any kind of pattern in verses 18-36 that shows us how to receive an ever increasing and growing witness?

Check out footnotes 24a, 26c, and 31a.

What do you think was the most impressive thing that Peter, James, and John heard, saw, and felt in verses 28-36?

Day 98, Luke 9:37-62

Earlier in this chapter Jesus gave His Apostles authority to heal (9:1) and they were successful (9:6). What do you think we are to learn from the Apostles failure to heal this boy (:40)?

Very rarely are our thoughts and feelings what they should be, and often we misunderstand. As you read today watch for examples of the Lord helping people who misunderstand, and how He helps them move toward understanding.

Today, watch for thoughts and feelings from the Holy Ghost to correct things we may misunderstand.

Day 99, Luke 10:1-24

In verses 1-20, Jesus calls the Seventy and gives them their charge. What does Jesus tell the Seventy that applies to us, and what is specifically just for them?

Which city will you be like? What good is a city, a town, or a person unless they receive the message and miracles, and repent?

What do verses 17-20 teach us about what types of things we should rejoice over?

Day 100, Luke 10:25-42

What new thoughts come to you if you apply the following symbolism to the parable of the Good Samaritan (:25-37)? Jerusalem = the premortal life; Jericho = the world; thieves = sin, temptations, and struggles; priest = the

Law of Moses; Levite = the prophets (this does not mean that they don't care, it only means that they cannot save us); Samaritan = Jesus Christ; Bound up, wine and oil = the Atonement and ordinances; inn = the Church; repay thee = eternal reward.

What do you think the message of Mary and Martha's story is in verses 38-42?

What types of "Mary and Martha" moments will you face today?

Day 101, Luke 11:1-28

Jesus' disciples asked him to teach them how to pray (:1). What subtle and significant thing does Jesus teach us about prayer in verses 2-13?

Casting out devils is a regular miracle for the Savior and His disciples. How does Mosiah 3:6 help us understand how this may also be a common miracle in our day?

How much power do devils have if it only takes the "finger of God" to cast them out (:20)?

Day 102, Luke 11:29-54

What do verses 34-36 teach us about our desires and priorities?

The Pharisees, scribes, and lawyers were all religious. What warnings does Jesus give to religious people in verses 42-52?

Footnote 52c helps us understand what the "fullness of knowledge" is.

Day 103, Luke 12:1-31

In verses 1-12, look for what the Savior teaches us about what we should and should not be afraid of.

What does the Savior teach in verses 13-31 about the position that possessions should play in our life? Why do you think these teachings are more relevant now than in Jesus' day?

Sometimes a single verse contains a whole talk. Which of these verses do you think is the greatest sermon in a single verse: 2, 4, 15, 23, 27, 28, or 31?

Day 104, Luke 12:32-59

Do you think we are really being honest with ourselves about what our treasures are? How do you think a person goes about changing what they treasure?

To believe in Christ means we expect some waiting. Waiting for prayers to be answered, waiting for ourselves or others to change, and waiting for the Second Coming. As you read verses 35-48 look for what Jesus teaches about why we wait, and what we should be doing while we wait.

We have all experienced verses 49-53, but why do you think Jesus taught it and what do you think we are supposed to do with it?

Day 105, Luke 13:1-17

In verses 1-5 Jesus teaches about repentance. What does the parable in verses 6-9 also teach us about repentance?

How has Jesus helped you do something that you could not do on your own (:11)?

Sometimes we may feel that the Sabbath day is full of restrictions. In verses 10-17 Jesus teaches that the Sabbath day is to help us be loosed from our burdens. In what ways have you ever felt, or seen someone loosed from their burdens or bonds because of the Sabbath day?

Day 106, Luke 13:17-35

Jesus knew that all His teachings and life would culminate with His experience in Jerusalem. Thus He worked, walked, and taught "toward Jerusalem" (:22). What would happen if we headed toward the Atonement as committedly as Jesus did?

As you read verses 23-30 look for reasons why more don't make it through the strait gate.

What is the result of not accepting the different ways the Savior can help us according to verses 34-35?

Day 107, Luke 14:1-24

What do you think are some opportunities that you will have this week to apply what the Savior teaches about pride and humility in verses 7-11?

Why is it important for us to care about and find ways to give to the poor, the unhealthy, and the unpopular?

The parable of the great supper found in verses 15-24 is about how the Lord makes invitations for people to attend, and how those who are invited make excuses for not coming. The precursor to the great supper of the Lord, which will come one day, is our weekly partaking of the sacrament. Which excuses pulls and tugs more at you: work (:18-19), or family (:20)? Work and family are both important, but if we make excuses then we will have no excuse (:24). Will you accept the Savior's invitation this week?

Day 108, Luke 14:25-35

Why do you think it is important to have the decision to keep the commandments "settled in . . . [our] hearts" (:27a)? Which commandments are settled and unsettled in your heart?

The other day someone told me they don't like the idea of just enduring. In verses 28-33, and 30a look for what Jesus teaches us about enduring discipleship.

What does Jesus teach about his relationship to prophets in footnote 34a?

Day 109, Luke 15:1-10

In response to those who questioned His choice of association, Jesus taught two parables in verses 3-7 and 8-10 to help everyone understand the value of every individual. As you read these parables look for: What was lost? Why it was lost? How was it found? What was the reaction when it was found?

What do these parables teach us about: How people become lost? How to find those who are lost? How does Heaven feel about the returning lost?

Do you think you are the one who is lost, looking, or both?

Day 110, Luke 15:11-32

What are the lessons that each son had to learn and how can those lessons help us?

What can the father in this story teach us about both mortal and eternal parenthood?

In what ways has your understanding and appreciation for this parable deepened over the years?

For more, check out Elder Holland's April 2002 Conference talk "The Other Prodigal".

Day 111, Luke 16

Notice the word "steward" and "stewardship" in verses 1-8.

Verses 1-8 tell about the parable of the unjust steward, and verses 9-13 are what we are to learn from this parable. Which verse best describes what you learned from the parable?

Which of the following do you think is the most important lesson we are to learn from the parable of the rich man and Lazarus (:19-31)? 1. Christianity must involve kindness to the poor. 2. Before Christ's death there was a "great gulf fixed" between the righteous and the wicked in the spirit world (:26). 3. Those that are dead are concerned and mindful of those who are alive (:27-28). 4. If people will not listen to prophets they would not listen to an angel or a dead relative either (:28-31).

Day 112, Luke 17:1-19

Verses 1-4 teach us about offense and forgiveness. Here are two of my favorite quotes about those subjects. Brigham Young supposedly said: "He who takes offense when no offense is intended is a fool, and he who takes offense when offense is intended is a greater fool." (Hanks, Marion D. "Forgiveness: The Ultimate Form of Love" *Ensign*. Jan, 1974). "Not forgiving is like drinking poison and expecting the other person to die."— Unknown.

The disciples ask for the Lord to teach them to increase their faith (:5). Why do you think the Savior responds to them by teaching what he does in verses 6-10?

What does the story in verses 11-19 dramatically teach you about being grateful and thankful? What has God done for you in the last few days, that you may not have noticed otherwise, that it would be good for you to be grateful for?

Day 113, Luke 17:20-37

If we could, we, like the Pharisees, might demand to know when the millennium will come. How can Jesus' answer in verses 20-21, and footnotes 21b, and 21c change the way that you view the coming of the kingdom of God? What will you do today to have the kingdom of God "among" or "within you?"

To help us better understand verse 32 I'm going to give several little quotes from a January, 2010 *Ensign* Article by Elder Jeffrey R. Holland, "The Best Is Yet To Be."

"'Remember Lot's wife.' What did He mean by such an enigmatic little phrase?"

"In short, her attachment to the past outweighed her confidence in the future."

"I plead with you not to dwell on days now gone, nor to yearn vainly for yesterdays, however good those yesterdays may have been. The past is to be learned from but not lived in. And when we have learned what we need to learn and have brought with us the best that we have experienced, then we look ahead and remember that faith is always pointed toward the future."

"She doubted the Lord's ability to give her something better than she already had. Apparently, she thought that nothing that lay ahead could possibly be as good as what she was leaving behind."

"There is something in many of us that particularly fails to forgive and forget earlier mistakes in life—either our mistakes or the mistakes of others. It is not good. It is not Christian."

"God doesn't care nearly as much about where you have been as He does about where you are and, with His help, where you are willing to go. That is the thing Lot's wife didn't get."

How does footnote 37a help us understand verses 34-37?

Day 114, Luke 18:1-23

As you read verses 1-8, look for the difference between how God and man answer petitions made to them.

In verses 9-14 look for the two different ways that these men approached worship. This week will you approach your church meetings, prayers, gospel study, and family activities with pride or humility?

What do you think enabled the Savior to see the children different than His disciples? Who do you need to view differently today?

Here we have a young man who has kept all of the basic commandments since he was a youth and now Jesus asks him to increase his discipleship (:18-23). Are you, like this young man, afraid of incrementally increasing your discipleship?

Day 115, Luke 18:24-43

When the disciples heard what Jesus said about the rich they thought that salvation might be impossible (:24-26). You may also feel that the struggles, problems, sins, and circumstances of your life are impossible to change, better, or be saved from. That is why we must remember verse 27.

Sometimes we feel that we have to leave home, family, and friends too often to attend meetings and fulfill callings. In verses 28-30 the Savior makes promises to all who at times leave. One these promises is "manifold more in this present time" (:30). I love that one of the purposes of every meeting that we will attend is to make our present condition better. How will you be a better husband/wife, mother/father, or son/daughter after your next meeting?

There are times when people will tell you to be quiet about your beliefs or make you feel uncomfortable. What would have happened to the blind man if he would have listened to those opposing voices in verses 35-43? How can this man's faith increase our courage?

Day 116, Luke 19:1-27

Verses 1-10 is a story for all of you who are vertically challenged. As you read these verses look for the effort that Zacchaeus put forth to come closer to his Savior, and things that could have kept him from trying.

What has been your sycamore tree this week?

Finish this statement: "If I put forth effort to get closer to the Savior, then He will..."

Many of the people at the time of Christ thought that the Second Coming and Millennium would happen soon (:11). In response to this belief Jesus gave the parable of the pounds (:12-27). The nobleman was only gone for one verse, (:14), the rest of the parable is about rendering accountability. How can this parable help us focus not on the time of the Second Coming, but on how we use our time until the Second Coming/day of accountability?

Day 117, Luke 19:28-48

The story of Jesus' disciples acquiring the colt is fascinating to me. Who do you think it would have been more uncomfortable to be, the disciples or the colt owners?

Sometimes the Lord asks us to go and ask others for their colts, and sometimes He sends others to ask us for our colts. When have there been times in your life when you have done one or the other of these things?

If we don't rejoice and testify of Christ, then the stones of the earth must (:39-40, see also D&C 88:88-90).

If Jesus knows the future of a city and weeps over it, and is willing to cleanse a temple that will be destroyed, then surely He also knows our future, weeps over, with us, and will cleanse us.

Day 118, Luke 20:1-26

Read the entire parable through once and try to understand what the Savior's story is saying (:9-19).

The Prophet Joseph Smith said, "I have a key by which I understand the scriptures. I enquire, what was the question which drew out the answer, or caused Jesus to utter the parable?" (*History of the Church*, 5:261). Now search through the verses before the parable (:1-8). Is there any help to teach us about what the question or reason for the parable was? This one is tough, but the parable is also taught in Matthew. Check out the JST for (Matthew 21:33) in the footnote.

Here are the major objects and actions in the parable. You may want to record what you think each represents: a certain man, vineyard, husbandmen, the servants, servants empty/beat/wounded, beloved son or heir, the son or heir killed and cast out, destroy the husbandmen, vineyard given to others, the stone that is rejected, the head of the corner.

The tribute money had Caesar's image on it. What do Genesis 1:26–27 and Alma 5:14 teach about where God's image should be? Based on what those scriptures teach what we should "render" to God? How are you going to do that today?

Day 119, Luke 20:27-47

In verses 27-39 Jesus speaking to a group of people who don't believe in the resurrection and marriage after death. What does He teach them about marriage? How can D&C 132:15-17 help us better understand Jesus' teachings?

They got to the point that they didn't want to learn, so they stopped asking questions. What questions and problems have you taken to Heavenly Father and Jesus Christ this week?

Day 120, Luke 21:1-19

Read verses 1-4 and look for what they can teach you about your calling, worship, and discipleship.

One of the most difficult things in life is learning how to speak carefully. What can we learn about how to do this from verses 14-15?

Verse 19 is worth your time to ponder. Also, check out 19b. How can this verse help us with daily challenges, failures, goals, and habits?

Day 121, Luke 21:20-38

Verses 20-24 contain a prophecy about the destruction of Jerusalem that occurred in 70 AD. Verses 25-38 gives us a prophecy about the Second Coming.

Here are some helpful footnotes 24f, 25a, 32a, 34a, and 36e.

Which of the following phrases do you think is most meaningful to you at this time: "Men's hearts failing them for fear" (:26), "Son of man coming...with power and great glory" (:27), "Look up and lift up your heads; for your redemption draweth nigh" (:28), "My words shall not pass away" (:33), "Your hearts overcharged with surfeiting" (:34), "And all the people came early in the morning to the temple for to hear him" (:38)?

Day 122 Luke 22:1-23

In your Bible Dictionary look up "feasts" and read paragraphs 1-6 to learn more about the Passover.

In this section of scripture we have the combination of the Passover and the Sacrament. The purpose of the Passover was to look back on the bondage and Exodus from Egypt and to look forward to the coming of the Messiah. The purpose of the Sacrament is to look back on the sacrifice of the Messiah and to look forward to the Second coming.

Exodus from Egypt ← Passover → **The Messiah** ← Sacrament → The Second Coming.

On a weekly basis how can you use the sacrament to look backwards and also forwards?

Peter and John were told to go and find a place to prepare the Passover (:8-9). The Passover was not something that could just be thrown together, they had to "make ready" (:12-13). The sacrament replaced the Passover. How will you prepare and make ready for the sacrament this week?

What difference does it make when you prepare and make ready for the sacrament each week?

Day 123, Luke 22:24-46

Today's section has several repeating themes. As you read, pay close attention and ponder these words: service, temptation, prayer, and strengthen.

As you studied and pondered over these themes, what thoughts or feelings increased your desire to pray, serve, or strengthen others?

Day 124, Luke 22:47-71

What do you think the difference is between Judas betraying Christ and Peter denying Christ?

Why do you think Peter was able to recover from this devastating night when Judas was not?

Hearing a testimony with only our ears does little good regardless who shares it (:67-71). What has helped you to hear the testimony of others with your ears and your heart?

Day 125, Luke 23:1-25

In what ways do you think this council of leaders thought Jesus was "perverting the nation" (:2)?

How have the teachings of Jesus stirred you up (:5)?

Read verses 11-12 and then finish the following sentence. Friendships forged by doing wrong things...

Day 126, Luke 23:26-53

During the most difficult 24 hours of his life, Jesus continually showed concern for others more than for himself (:28). What difference would it make during our difficult days if we tried to do the same?

Which of these things will you spend more time doing today: deriding, mocking, railing things and people, or forgiving people and their mistakes?

What can we learn from how each of the following groups or individuals reacted to the Savior? If He said something to them what was it, and why was it important?

Simon (:26)

The women (:27-31, 49, 54-56)

The malefactors (:32-33, 39-43)

The people (:35, 48)

The soldiers (:34, 36-38)

The centurion (:44-47)

Joseph (:50-53)

Day 127, Luke 24:1-35

The story in verse 1 will change the Sabbath from Saturday to Sunday.

Several people in these verses needed to gain a testimony about the resurrection. Carefully ponder all of the different ways that people had their testimonies increased in this section. Which of those has also helped you?

You just learned a lot about receiving a testimony, now ponder about what this section teaches us about sharing testimony with others. What did you learn?

Day 128, Luke 24:36-53

What can we learn about the nature of resurrected bodies from these verses?

"And while they yet believed not for joy, and wondered" (:41). How would you explain what this phrase means?

Look at these verses and footnotes 49, 49b, 53, 53a for what a person can do to prepare themselves to be "endued" with more spiritual power.

Day 129, John 1:1-34

Look up "John, Gospel of" in your Bible Dictionary for any additional details. One thing that you will notice is that John is writing to people who are familiar with the gospel and symbolism.

In verses 1-14 John the Beloved shares several powerful ideas about Jesus Christ. Which of these do you find most important?

Since John the Beloved shared his witness earlier, he now quotes the testimony of John the Baptist in verses 15-28. How many different times and ways does John the Baptist teach that Jesus is the promised one?

Verse 18 sometimes causes confusion for people, but footnotes 18a, b, and c, can be very helpful.

Day 130, John 1:35-51

In verses 35-51 we read the story about how John the Beloved and his friends gained a testimony of Jesus. Look for how John (who is one of the two disciples mentioned), Andrew, Simon, Philip, and Nathanael received their testimonies.

What does this story teach us about sharing the gospel with other people?

Did anyone in your life find you and help you to receive a belief in Jesus Christ?

Day 131, John 2

The wine that they used had some alcohol in it. Not enough to get anyone knee-walking drunk on, but some. Let's not impose our word of wisdom upon them. They got wine, but we get bacon.

The water that Jesus used was for "purifying" (:6). Look up "purification" in your Bible Dictionary, and then complete the following: If Christ can change purifying water into wine then he can...

A firkin is 8-9 gallons. That means Jesus made 100-150 gallons of wine. What does that amount teach us about the power of Christ and the Atonement's ability to cover our needs?

Day 132, John 3:1-15

Look for evidence that Nicodemus was sincere in his questions and investigation. Also look for how Jesus teaches about faith, repentance, baptism, the Holy Ghost, and the Atonement.

Notice how often the word "born" is used in verses 3-8.

How is the Spirit like the wind (:8)? We can't see it with our eyes. We can feel it. We can see its effects. It can be gentle, strong, or powerful.

Day 133, John 3:16-36

"The narrative of this interview between Nicodemus and the Christ constitutes one of our most instructive and precious scriptures relating to the absolute necessity of unreserved compliance with the laws and ordinances of the gospel, as the means indispensable to salvation .... Every line is of significance; the writer fully realized the deep import of his subject and treated it accordingly." (James E. Talmage, *Jesus The Christ*, p. 162-163).

Read John 3:16-22. What new significant thing did you discover?

The Mandaeans were a group of people who believed that John the Baptist was the Messiah and that Jesus was his disciple. They claim this because Jesus went to John to be baptized. In answer to this, John preaches one of the greatest sermons on Christ and His divinity. Read verses 27-36 and find places where John the Baptist did an awesome job at being a prophet, diminishing his own role while increasing Jesus'.

Day 134, John 4:1-26

This story is incredible. A woman comes to get water and leaves having heard the personal testimony of Christ, that He is the/her Messiah. How did Jesus help this woman shift from performing a necessary and routine task to thinking and talking about her beliefs, worship, and salvation?

What evidence is there that Jesus cared for this woman as an individual?

What can we learn from the conversation that Jesus and the Samaritan woman have about the proper/correct way and place to worship in verses 20-24? Look up "Samaritans" in the Bible Dictionary for additional understanding.

What do you think this woman felt when Jesus said verses 25-26?

Day 135, John 4:27-54

Look for what the Samaritan woman calls Jesus in verses 9, 11, 15, 19, and 29. What do you think led to each name change?

Using only names and titles, how would you express the change in your relationship to Jesus?

Is there anyone you worry about who lives in another place (:45-47)? Cana is thirteen miles straight or twenty-five miles on foot to Capernaum. Cana is 700 ft. above sea level. Capernaum is 700 ft. below sea level.

Whose faith do you think healed the child (:48-53)? Does distance matter? What if the towns were 200 or 2,000 miles apart? How can we apply this story to our friends that we are worried about?

Day 136, John 5:1-24

How did the miracle in verses 1-14 show the power of Christ and at the same time correct and eclipse superstitions and false religious traditions?

What can we learn about Heavenly Father and Jesus Christ from what is said about them in verses 17-24? What do you think is the most important thing that you learned about Heavenly Father or Jesus Christ?

Day 137, John 5:25-47

What do you think verses 25-29 say about the resurrection? These were the verses that Joseph Smith and Sidney Rigdon were translating and pondering on that led to the vision of the degrees of glory (D&C 76:15-18).

In the center of a piece of paper, write "Jesus Christ". As you read verses 30-47, write down all of the different things that witness that Jesus is the Christ like spokes on a wheel.

What other witnesses have you had that Jesus is the Christ? Add them to the others on your witness wheel.

I invite you to take time to share your thoughts and feeling about Jesus with the people that matter a lot to you so that you may become a spoke for them.

Day 138, John 6:1-21

Which do you think is the greater miracle: the feeding of the 5,000 or that a "lad" gave up his food for others (:9)? If Jesus can do that with this little offering, then what does that mean in regards to our little offerings and efforts?

Jesus Christ has power over deficiency. Whatever you are lacking in your life, the answer is to take what little you do have and offer it in faith to the Savior and He will multiply it. What are some of the different ways you have experienced this principle in your life?

Giving thanks for what we have always results in a greater forthcoming abundance (:11, and D&C 78:19).

If Jesus can multiply fish and bread, why do you think we have verse 12?

Day 139, John 6:22-40

Jesus mentions that this group of people did not seek Him out for the right reasons (:24-26, 26a). What do you think are the reasons that Jesus wants us to seek Him out?

For forty years the children of Israel were fed with manna from heaven which they had to gather daily. As you read verses 28-40, discover ways that Jesus is like manna. Also find ways in which Jesus is not like manna. What did you learn that could help you in your daily gathering/seeking of Jesus?

Day 140, John 6:41-71

Verses 41-59 are Jesus' attempt to help people move from a misunderstanding to a correct understanding about who He is and how important He is. What did the group misunderstand about Jesus? What did Jesus teach about His own significance?

Believing in Jesus is not always easy. He says things that can be challenging and even cause offense. What do verses 60-71 teach us about being confused, offended, and in doubt? What do these verses teach us about people leaving Christ and about people staying with Christ?

Day 141, John 7:1-27

Because of the miracles and the boldness of His teachings, everyone is talking about Jesus (:1-13, 25-27). What did Jesus' own brothers think of Him and what were others saying about Him? What were the last things that you said about Him? What will you say about Him next?

The people questioned Jesus' education and credentials because He did not attend the scribe schools. In response, Jesus taught them and us about how we can obtain true learning and growth (:14-19). Why do you think what Jesus taught is important?

The Sabbath day healings have angered some. To help them learn an important principle about righteous judgment Jesus pointed out that they circumcise people on the Sabbath to help them be faithful to the covenant (:19-24). How well do we judge righteously? Are we looking for what people do wrong or what they do right? Yes, that also would include looking at ourselves. How did this principle help you today?

Day 142, John 7:28-53

In today's section, there are several who believe that Jesus is the Christ and several who do not. What reasons did each group give? What reasons would you give for your belief that Jesus is the Christ?

This section is also a good one to visualize. As you read, consider the pace, the volume of the speech, and all of the "then"s that move the story along.

Verse 39 gives some very interesting insight on the Holy Ghost. Also see footnote 39a, and "Holy Ghost" in the Bible Dictionary.

Day 143, John 8:1-20

What does the story in verses 1-11 teach you about judgment, judging, repentance, and forgiveness?

In what ways was getting caught and brought to Jesus Christ the best possible thing that could have happened to this woman? In what ways can getting caught also be the best thing for us?

What do verses 12-20 help us to discover about the physicality of Heavenly Father and Jesus Christ and their relationship to each other?

Day 144, John 8:21-59

As you read, watch for what Jesus teaches about relationships: Him and Heavenly Father, Us and the Father, Us and Him, relationships to Abraham, and also relationships to the Devil. What did you learn about these important relationships?

In what ways has verse 32 been true and helpful in your life? Also check out these killer cross references, John 14:6 & D&C 93:24. What do these cross references add to your understanding of this verse?

In order to understand why the people were willing to stone Jesus to death in verse 59, we have to understand what He was really saying in verse 58. Footnote 58b is key.

Day 145, John 9:1-23

What types of blindness can you see in today's section? What do you think made the difference between who was and who wasn't healed of their blindness?

What do verses 1-3 teach us about assigning blame for our misfortunes and difficulties in this life?

I love that Jesus put mud in, or on this man's eyes, as part of his healing. Sometimes we also need to wash the mud/world out or our vision.

Day 146, John 9:24-41

Today we continue the story of the man born blind from birth. The Pharisees have called him back for questioning. There is some excellent dialogue in this section. If you read it out loud you will get more out of it.

This man is cast out because of his experience in being cured. What do you think is the most impressive thing that happens when Jesus learns that this man has been cast out (:35-38)?

Since we have begun our study of Jesus, what kinds of things do you see differently (:39)? How has your vision been improved?

The man's eyes were healed because of the kindness of Jesus. What did the man do after that led to the healing of his soul?

Day 147, John 10:1-21

What principles or truths can we learn about leadership, parenting, and even business from today's reading?

I have a deep love for verse 10. In what ways has Christ and His teachings made your life more abundant recently?

It is through His parental pedigree that Jesus obtained both of the abilities mentioned in verses 17-18.

Checkout footnote 16a for an additional connection.

Day 148, John 10:22-42

Verse 24 contains a question. Read verses 25-39 and look for the different ways that Jesus answers their question, and how they respond?

There are two similar phrases used in verses 28-29. Why do you think it is significant that we will not be plucked out of the Father's and Jesus' hand?

In verses 30-39 Jesus teaches a doctrine and the people are ready to stone him for it. What did Jesus teach about God, Himself, and ourselves that caused people to want to kill him?

Day 149, John 11:1-29

Thomas is best remembered as "Doubting Thomas," who said that he would not believe in the resurrection of Christ until he had seen and touched Him. Not his best moment. His best moment is verse 16. He believes Jesus will be killed if they go to Jerusalem and Thomas is ready to go and to die with Him. Why do you think it is important to remember the best of people rather than their worst?

The Jews believed that the spirit of a deceased person stays near the body for three days (:17). In other words, Lazarus is "all dead" and not "mostly dead". This makes the miracle more impressive, and a definitive witness of Jesus' divine power.

In verses 19-28 look for all of the different ways that Martha demonstrates her faith in Christ. How will you demonstrate your faith in Christ today?

Day 150, John 11:30-57

Verse 35 is the shortest in all of the scriptures. Do you think this verse is significant or simply informative?

Jesus knew he was going to raise Lazarus from the dead. Why then do you suppose He wept? What can we learn about how to handle mortal death from this?

In what ways can death help strengthen our faith in Christ? When have you experienced faith in Christ's resurrection that helped you in the event of someone's death?

Look for how the Jewish leaders reacted to this miracle in verses 47-54. What was the solution they decided on?

Day 151, John 12:1-26

What can we learn by comparing Mary and Judas in verses 1-8?

On this occasion, with his death approaching, Jesus Christ gladly received this preferential treatment. What does His comment in verse 8 say about our relationship to and treatment of Jesus and the poor?

In addition to Jesus, look for who else's life is now in danger and why (:9-11)?

Jesus and His ministry become more significant over time (:16). When have you experienced some small event in your past becoming more and more significant?

Day 152, John 12:27-50

Hearing a voice out of heaven is never a light thing, therefore read verses 27-30 carefully and look for what this voice said, and why it came.

What does the Savior say about belief and disbelief in verses 32-50?

Which do you think is easier, to believe or to disbelieve and why?

Day 153, John 13:1-20

The Last Supper included eating the Passover, partaking of the sacrament, Judas being identified as the one who would betray Christ, and the washing of the feet.

Search verses 1-17 for a couple of reasons that Jesus gives this act of service to His disciples.

D&C 88:138-140 is a great cross reference for the washing of the feet.

"The house of the Lord must be prepared, and the solemn assembly called and organized in it, according to the order of the house of God; and in it we must attend to the ordinance of washing of feet. It was never intended for any but official members. It is calculated to unite our hearts, that we may be one in feeling and sentiment, and that our faith may be strong, so that Satan cannot overthrow us, nor have any power over us here." (Joseph Smith, *Teachings*, 91).

Jesus is our "example" in all things (:15). How will you follow His example today?

Day 154, John 13:21-38

"Judas was rebuked and immediately betrayed his Lord into the hands of His enemies, because Satan entered into him (:2, 21-30). There is a superior intelligence bestowed upon such as obey the Gospel with full purpose of heart, which, if sinned against, the apostate is left naked and destitute of the Spirit of God ... When once that light which was in them is taken from them, they become as much darkened as they were previously enlightened." (Joseph Smith, *Teachings*, 67).

Jesus knew that Judas would betray Him, yet He washed his feet. What does the Savior's example teach you about how we are to treat those that we struggle with or who don't like us?

Why do you think it is so important to our Heavenly Father and Jesus Christ that we love one another (:32-34)? Look at verse 35 for a result and blessing of love. How do you develop this love if you don't feel like you have it? Why do you think it is called a new commandment?

Day 155, John 14

If the Apostles knew that this was the last night that they would have with Jesus before He left them, what questions or concerns do you think they would have?

Read each of the following sections looking for what direction or comfort the Lord gives to His Apostles and you.

Verses 1-6

Verses 12-15

Verses 16-17, 26-27

Verses 18-24

Day 156, John 15

Today's chapter has several themes. Read the chapter, then write down a truth that you learned for each one of these words:

fruit

abide

love

servants

friends

hate

Day 157, John 16

In verses 1-6, Jesus tells the Apostles that after He leaves, they will die. In verses 7-15 He speaks of the Holy Ghost. In verses 16-22 Jesus speaks of this life before the Second Coming. Then in verses 23-26 He speaks of the Millennium. Finally, Jesus bears His testimony to His disciples in verses 27-32. In verse 33 Jesus tells his disciples that what He has spoken to them is to help them have peace in this world. Therefore, as you read this chapter, consider how these teachings can help bring peace to your hardships, stresses, and sorrows.

In verse 7 Jesus told His Apostles that He must leave them so that He can send them the Holy Ghost. Read verses 8-15 and look for what the Holy Ghost does that is so important that Jesus leaves so that this could happen.

What does verse 12 teach you about receiving revelation?

Day 158, John 17

Read verses 1-3 and then read this quote: "We should go far beyond knowing about Jesus and about his attributes and mission. We should come to 'know ... the only true God, and Jesus Christ, whom thou hast sent' (John 17:3). It is one thing to know about God and another to know him ... But we know them, in the sense of gaining eternal life, when we enjoy and experience the same things they do. To know God is to think what he thinks, to feel what he feels, to have the power he possesses, to comprehend the truths he understands, and to do what he does. Those who know God become like him, and have his kind of life, which is eternal life." (Joseph B. Wirthlin, "Our Lord and Savior," *Ensign*, Nov. 1993, 5)

President David O. McKay said of John 17: "I know of no more important chapter in the Bible" (*Conference Report*, Oct. 1967, 5).

This chapter is a prayer known as the great "Intercessory Prayer" or Jesus' prayer for us. Read John 17 and look for how Jesus feels about you and what He wants for you.

Day 159, John 18:1-18

Jesus went often to the garden where He performed the Atonement (:1-2). How often do you think Jesus wants us to think about or use what He did in that garden? How often do you go to the garden and the Atonement? If you will go to the garden and the Atonement today by asking for help and strength with your struggles and stresses, you will receive the strength sufficient for the day.

Notice this phrase "And Judas also, which betrayed him, stood with them" (:5). When we are faced with choices it is helpful to ask the question: Who do I or who will I stand with?

Remembering who we are and why we are here is essential. As you read today's section, see what examples you can discover of Jesus never forgetting and Peter momentarily forgetting who he was and why he was here.

Day 160, John 18:19-40

We are going to continue to look for examples of Jesus remembering who He was and how that gave Him strength. Also look for examples of Peter and the Jewish leaders forgetting who they are.

The Jewish Leaders didn't defile themselves by entering into the hall of gentiles, but by allowing evil to enter into the hall of their hearts (:28). They sought to keep the laws of the Romans, but not the laws of God. Whose people had they become (:31)? Finally, they even choose a murderous criminal over the innocent Christ (:38-40). We shouldn't choose lies and wickedness over Christ. We would rather have evil in our lives than the Son of God. How often do we choose friends, fads, and filth over the Son of God?

Day 161, John 19:1-22

As you read, discover what reasons Pilot had to let Jesus go and what reasons he had to crucify Him.

What does Pilot misunderstand about his own power in verses 10-11?

What was the controversy concerning the sign on the cross in verses 19-22? What sign would you have hung up?

Day 162, John 19:23-42

John, like Matthew, pointed out several events in the Savior's life that were prophesied of in ancient scripture (:23-24, 24a; 31-37, 36a).

It is very interesting that Jesus selected John the Beloved to take care of his mother Mary (:25-27). John, because of his righteous desires, would be blessed with power over death until the Second Coming of the Savior (John 21:20-24, D&C 7). If you were Jesus who else would you pick?

It was only after the needs of all others were met, and the Atonement safely accomplished, that Jesus then requested something for Himself (:28). Today we invite you to attempt to put the needs of others above your own just a little bit more.

Day 163, John 20

As you read this chapter look for how and when each person started to believe in Christ's resurrection.

John concludes this chapter by telling us why he wrote all these things in verses 30-31. Do you think he was successful? When and how did you start to believe in Christ's resurrection?

What is your favorite part about the story of Mary in verses 1-18?

Footnote 17a changes the language from "touch me not" to "hold me not" which is closer to the Greek translation which says "stop holding me" or "stop embracing me", because He had to go to the Father.

Twice the resurrected Savior appeared and proclaimed "peace be unto you" (:21, 26). In what ways has the resurrection brought peace unto you?

Day 164, John 21

Anything that we might say about verses 1-17 is said better in Elder Holland's talk, "The First Great Commandment." Read it and be moved to take action (Elder Jeffrey R. Holland, "The First Great Commandment" *General Conference* Oct 2012, or *Ensign,* Nov 2012).

Look for what is going to happen to Peter in verses 18-19, and John in verses 20-23. Who would you rather be?

There may be places that we don't want to go, or things that we don't want to do: mission, temple, church, institute, mutual, fast offerings, priesthood. What is the Savior saying in verses 19 and 20 to us who have been asked to do things that we don't want to?

Day 165, Acts 1

"Indeed, a more complete title for the book of Acts could appropriately be something like 'The Acts of the Resurrected Christ Working through the Holy Spirit in the Lives and Ministries of His Ordained Apostles.' Now, having said that, you can see why someone voted for the shorter title—but my suggested title is more accurate!" (Elder Jeffrey R. Holland "Therefore What" Aug 8th 2000, p.6).

The book of Acts is a record of the Apostles acting under the direction of Christ as he administers his Church through the Holy Ghost. There are 240 references in scripture about the Holy Ghost, 41 are in the book of Acts. That is more than any other, with 3 Nephi at 26, D&C 20 at 9, and the 4 gospels at 26. (Acts 1:2, 5, 8, 16; 2:4; 4:8, 31; 5:3, 32; 6:3, 5; 7:51, 55; 8:15, 17, 18, 19; 9:17, 31; 10:38, 44-47; 11:15, 16, 24; 13:2, 4, 9, 52; 15:8, 28; 16:6; 19:2, 6; 20:23, 28; 21:11; 28:25). There are also an additional 16 references made about the Spirit: (2:4, 17, 18; 5:9; 6:10; 8:29, 39; 10:19; 11:12, 28; 16:7; 18:5; 19:21, 20:22; 21:4). There is hardly anything that happens in this book without the Holy Ghost being involved.

In verses 1-13 look for what promises Jesus makes to his Apostles, and for what the angels wanted the Apostles to know about Christ's ascension.

Since Judas has died, there are only 11 Apostles (:13-20). What can we learn about the calling of a new Apostle from verses 21-26? "Lots" means votes, or sustaining.

Day 166, Acts 2:1-21

Pentecost or the feast of weeks is celebrated 50 days after the feast of Passover. During this time the grain harvest began. This feast is characterized by meal offerings, and 2 loaves of leavened bread. This feast also commemorated God giving the Torah, or the law to the children of Israel on Mount Sinai. To Christians the day of Pentecost has also come to commemorate the Apostles receiving the Holy Ghost.

In verses 2-4 look for how they describe this experience with the Holy Ghost. Can you think of a time when you powerfully felt the Holy Ghost? What words would you use to describe your experience?

The seventh Article of Faith declares our belief in the gift of tongues. The experience in verses 5-21 share a perfect example that the primary purpose of that spiritual gift is to teach the gospel to those of a different language. Notice how many different languages were spoken and also what happened with those who didn't have a spiritual experience.

Day 167, Acts 2:22-47

What does Peter, using many of the words of King David, say about Christ in verses 22-36?

What effect did Peter's testimony have on those listening according to verses 37-41? When have you been greatly affected by someone's testimony, or affected someone else with yours?

In verses 42-47 look for what was similar about the Church then and now?

Day 168, Acts 3

What do you think is the best thing said, and the best thing done in verses 1-11?

President Harold B. Lee said: "Peter just didn't content himself by commanding the man to walk, but he 'took him by the right hand, and lifted him up ... that chiefest of the apostles, perhaps with his arms around the shoulders of the man, and saying, 'Now, my good man, have courage. I will take a few steps with you. Let's walk together... Then the man leaped with joy. You cannot lift another soul until you are standing on higher ground than he is. You must be sure, if you would rescue the man, that you yourself are setting the example of what you would have him be. You cannot light a fire in another soul unless it is burning in your own." (Stand Ye in Holy Places, Deseret Book, 1974, pp. 186-87.)

Who has played the role of Peter in your life? What must you do so that you can play the role of Peter in someone else's life?

Read verses 12-26 and choose what you think are the three most important phrases in Peter's testimony to the Jews.

Day 169, Acts 4:1-22

Because many people believed the testimony of Peter, he and John are arrested for healing the lame man in Acts 3. The next day Peter and John are taken before many of the same people who conspired against Jesus. Peter's boldness is undeniable, but he was also "filled with the Holy Ghost" (:8). As you read Peter's bold testimony in verses 8-12 watch for the parts that fill you with the Holy Ghost.

In verses 13-22 you will see the reaction to Peter's testimony. Do you stand with the apostles or just wish that they would stop speaking (:14, 18)?

How could you be bolder in your declarations of belief in Jesus Christ?

Day 170, Acts 4:23-37

In the previous section, Peter and John were threatened to not talk about their experience healing the lame man. Why do you think they responded like they did (:23-31)?

When have you felt that kind of witness from an Apostle like the one described in verse 33?

What can we learn about how our donations are used to bless others from verses 34-37? What donations have you laid at the Apostles feet that they now use to bless others?

Day 171, Acts 5:1-21

When someone sits down to talk with a Bishop about going to the temple what kinds of questions does the Bishop ask? Which ones do you think people are tempted to lie about?

Search the scripture story in verses 1-11 for lessons that we can learn. Did you find anything troubling/disturbing about this story? Do people always suffer the consequence for lying?

"In our time those found in dishonesty do not die as did Ananias and Sapphira, but something within them dies. Conscience chokes, character withers, self-respect vanishes, integrity dies" (Gordon B. Hinckley. *Ensign,* May 1976, 61).

What would you tell someone who is worried about being honest with their Bishop, parents, others, or themselves?

Day 172, Acts 5:22-42

Which of these news stories would get your attention?

1. Church members seek for shadow healings (:12-16).

2. Apostles of the Church jailed for a 2nd time (:17-18).

3. Jail break to temple teaching (:19-26).

4. Preaching while being told not to preach (:27-32).

Verse 13 says that the Apostles performed many signs and wonders. What signs and wonders have you had in your life?

Gamaliel was a great leader and doctor of the law. He told the other Jewish leaders, who were troubled because of Peter, a way to discover if the Christian movement was of God or not. Look for what advice he gave to discover if something is of God or not in verses 33-40.

Day 173, Acts 6:1-15

What was the problem? What was the solution? How well did the solution work?

In what ways can you be, or have you been a solution to the same problem?

Day 174, Acts 7:1-21

Stephen is put in prison on false charges. He begins his defense by brilliantly summarizing the Old Testament. What does this quick summary teach you about God's promises? In what ways can that principle relate to the promises in your patriarchal blessing?

Why do you think it is important for a person to believe the truths mentioned in verses 9-10?

Day 175, Acts 7:22-43

Stephen continues his summary of the Old Testament by telling of Moses and the Exodus from Egypt. Verses 22-29 speak of Moses' initial rejection, verses 30-38 are about Moses' selection by God, and verses 39-43 deal with apostasy in the wilderness. In verse 37 Moses makes a prophecy of a prophet that will be like him. This prophet is Christ. As you read each of these sections about Moses' life look for ways in which Moses symbolizes Christ.

Moses was raised speaking Egyptian not Hebrew (:22). This may be a reason of why Moses was afraid to speak and needed Aaron (Exodus 4:10-16).

The phrase "lively oracles" means living prophets (:38). While Moses was up on Mount Sinai receiving God's commandments, the children of Israel built a golden idol to worship. We are given a warning in modern revelation concerning the living oracles (D&C 90:5). Why do you think people ancient and modern preferred idols, philosophies, or other beliefs that don't speak and correct them over living prophets? What is the difference you have experienced in adhering to the living oracles and not just the dead ones?

Day 176, Acts 7:44-60

Ancient Israel had several things that modern Israel has: temples, prophets, scriptures, the Holy Ghost, the Law, and commandments. As you read verses 44-53. look how those resources were used.

How do you respond when you are corrected or cut to your heart (:54)?

Because he was full of the Holy Ghost, Stephen was able to see a vision before his death (:55-56). What do you find remarkable about this vision?

Day 177, Acts 8:1-25

In this section we read about Saul, Philip, Simon, Peter, and John. Pay attention to what type of power each had.

What can today's section teach us about increasing and decreasing spiritual power?

What experiences have you had in your life that demonstrates that there really is a power in the gift of the Holy Ghost?

Day 178, Acts 8:26-40

What does Philip teach us about how to be a good teacher and missionary?

This Ethiopian eunuch was important enough that the Lord had an angel tell Philip to go to the desert to teach him, and then Philip is conveyed away when the eunuch was converted. What does this teach you about how important each individual is?

Have you had a miraculous moment in your life when the Lord used you to reach out and help an individual?

Day 179, Acts 9:1-22

Saul and Ananias both receive assignments from the Lord. What do you think could have made either assignment difficult?

How does the way these two men responded to their assignments make you feel about the difficult things that have been assigned to you?

Day 180, Acts 9:23-43

Saul is trying to change his life, and that can be very hard. As you read verses 23-31 watch for things that made life difficult for our new convert.

What are some of the difficulties new members or returning members may face? How could we do a better job acting like the disciples who lowered Saul in the basket?

In verses 32-43 you will see that Peter has become a powerful miracle performer. Notice the results of these miracles, and the similarities between them and ones performed by Jesus.

Day 181, Acts 10:1-23

In today's section we will read two visions, one by the prophet Peter and the other by Cornelius. Cornelius' vision is in verses 1-8. As you read it, look for what he did that helped prepare him to receive this vision. Peter's experience is found in verses 9-23. As you read it, look for what Peter does after his spiritual experience to help him better understand it.

What do you think we are to learn from the facts that the revelation didn't come all at once, and that it involved multiple people receiving promptings and acting on it?

Day 182, Acts 10:24-48

Because of Cornelius' dream Peter has come to his house despite the fact that he is of another nation and a gentile (:28). This is a great act of faith and humility for Peter. Look for what Peter teaches is and isn't important to God in verses 34-43.

Verses 44-48 can sometimes cause confusion because the Holy Ghost comes upon this group that Peter teaches before they are baptized. For help understanding this look up "Holy Ghost" in the Bible Dictionary. What is the difference between the gift and the power of the Holy Ghost?

Day 183, Acts 11

Look up "Gentile" in Bible Dictionary.

What similarities do you see between the Gospel being preached to the Gentiles for the first time and the lifting of the temple and priesthood restriction with regard to race?

There are always needs and causes to donate to. How does a person know how much they should give? Verse 29 gives us a great guide for this.

Day 184, Acts 12

This chapter is a paradox. What lessons can we learn from James' death and Peter's miraculous deliverance?

Many people are unsure about the reality of angels and their ministry in our lives. This chapter is unequivocal in its declaration that angels and their ministry are real. I declare my belief in angels, and their seen and unseen daily help. My family has been a recipient of such ministries and we thank God for His angels.

Day 185, Acts 13:1-25

In verses 1-5 notice how Luke, the author of the book of Acts, points out all of the spiritual preparation for missionary calls and service.

When Paul's perspective convert's faith is shaken by a sorcerer watch for what Paul does in verses 6-12 to establish the truthfulness of the gospel message. Why do you think this is not as a common of an approach today?

While preaching to a group in a synagogue on the Sabbath day, Paul recounts the Old Testament as a lead up to Jesus Christ. In verses 16-25 notice all of the verbs associated with God in these verses.

Day 186, Acts 13:26-52

In verses 26-40, Paul declares that the prophecies and promises of the Old Testament are fulfilled through Jesus Christ. Watch for the old witnesses and the new witnesses.

Paul's whole sermon comes down to verses 38-39. No obedience to any law or sacrifice can justify our wrongs or forgive us. Have you experienced the justification and forgiveness that comes through Belief in Christ? When more wrongs come, know also that so will the forgiveness.

Paul's speech in verses 41-52 divides the people into believers and scoffers. Why does the gospel demand that you pick a side? Why do you think Paul and Barnabas could be happy even when they and their message was rejected?

Day 187, Acts 14

In verses 1-7, the pattern of preaching and rejection is repeated. How relevant do you think verses 2-4 are today?

In verses 8-18, what miracle does Paul perform that leads many to think that he and Barnabas are gods? What does Paul mean when he attempts to correct this misunderstanding by saying "We also are men of like passions with you" (:15)?

Please don't read quickly over verses 19-20. Is this experience different from the near death experiences that you or others have had?

Day 188, Acts 15:1-23

In this chapter there is a dispute about the Gentiles and circumcision. Look for the following pattern for solving doctrinal disputes as you read today's section: First, discover the problem, or ask a question. Second, bring it to church leaders who will meet in council to consider the problem. Third, the members of the council discuss and dispute the matter. Fourth, the Prophet/President explains what the Lord has revealed on the subject. Fifth, other leaders speak to sustain the counsel of the President and confirm that it was of God. Sixth, the decision of the council is sent out to the rest of the Church members.

Is there anything wrong with having questions about Church doctrines or policies?

Why do you think asking questions is an essential part of the process of receiving revelation?

What if we don't understand something that the prophets ask us to do?

Day 189, Acts 15:22-41

Following the council about the Gentiles, the Apostles united on the decision, then letters and messengers are sent forth (:22-29). Notice that this ultimately comes from the Holy Ghost (:28).

How do modern prophets and apostles communicate their decisions to us today? What do we do if we don't understand something that the apostles ask us to do? What do we do if we don't agree with what they have told us?

What experiences have you had in following the decisions of prophets that has caused you to trust them?

Day 190, Acts 16:1-18

Paul's 2nd mission started in Acts 15:36 and will run through Acts 18:23. In verses 1-5 Paul has Timothy circumcised so that he can teach both Jews and Gentiles the gospel. What have you done to be more versatile at sharing the gospel with others?

In your maps, look at the missionary journeys of Paul. This is a lot of traveling. What do verses 6-10 say about why Paul went where he did? What does that teach you about your own missionary efforts?

In verses 13-18, we see two women who become convinced through different sources that Paul and his companions are servants of God. Why do you think Paul thought it was important that people come to believe that they are servants because of a change of heart and not through a paid diviner?

Day 191, Acts 16:19-40

Yesterday, Paul cast a spirit out of a slave woman. Look for what reasons were given in verses 19-24 for throwing Paul into prison.

A prison break is maybe the worst possible thing that could happen to a jailer. How did this turn into a blessing in verses 25-34? How have you seen the gospel change terrible situations into blessings?

These leaders beat what they thought was a foreigner, and now Paul informed them that he is a Roman citizen. To unfairly imprison and beat a Roman citizen could mean death. The keeper of the prison counseled Paul to "go in peace" (:36). Why is that good counsel for when we have been mistreated?

Day 192, Acts 17:1-15

Paul's teaching is described as "reasoned with them out of the scriptures" (:2). In what ways do you think that is different from simply reading the scriptures?

Later while teaching in Berea, Paul and Silas find a people who "received the word with all readiness of mind, and searched the scriptures daily" (:11). Why could each of these phrases or words be important: "readiness of mind", "searched", and "daily"?

Today's whole section is about how two groups of saints came to believe because of the proper use of the scriptures. How well are you doing at using the scriptures in the way that these saints did?

Day 193, Acts 17:16-34

What kinds of things did the people of Athens say about Paul in verses 16-21? What would you say is the difference between philosophy and religion?

For fear of offending an unknown God the people of Athens built an altar to an unknown God and made sacrifices. Look for what Paul says in this incredible sermon about who God really is in verses 22-31.

Which doctrine mentioned in verses 32-34 caused the people of Athens not to listen to Paul anymore? Why do you think this doctrine caused them to stop listening to Paul?

Day 194, Acts 18

In verse 3, check out what Paul did to make money.

It is very discouraging to put forth diligent effort in preaching and teaching the gospel only to watch as people reject it. Look for what Paul said and did when he was in that situation in verses 1-8.

In verses 9-10 Paul has a vision of the Lord who says several things to encourage him. Which of these phrases do you personally need at this time to encourage you?

You've most likely noticed that Paul travels a lot. In verse 23 we learn why Paul travels so much. In all his endeavors he is trying to strengthen people. We have a great example of this in the story of Apollos, who is already great, but through the ministries of Aquila and Priscillia became an even greater strength (:24-28). Who will you strengthen today?

Day 195, Acts 19:1-20

What significant and subtle things does the story in verses 1-7 teach us about baptism and the Holy Ghost?

Check out the kind of special miracles performed by Paul in verses 11-12?

What does this funny and frightening story in verses 13-20 help us understand about authority and power?

Day 196, Acts 19:22-41

Paul's teaching sometimes engendered feelings of dislike. In verses 23-29 look for reasons why the group of people struggled accepting the gospel message. What are some of the reasons: work, beliefs, political ideals, or experiences, that make accepting the gospel a difficult choice for people?

A silver guild has incited a confused riot (:32). Look for what several different people do to defuse the ill feelings that have arisen between these different groups in verses 33-41. What can we learn from these men to help us not to be disagreeable to those with whom we disagree?

Why do you think it is important to learn how to get along with people who feel and believe different than we do?

Day 197, Acts 20:1-16

Sunday became the established day for partaking of the sacrament (:7).

The next time you are getting sleepy listening to a talk in church remember verses 7-12. This is not just a close call, but a miracle.

What do you think the phrase "not a little comforted" means (:12)? What experiences have you had that have left you feeling the same way?

Day 198, Acts 20:17-38

Today's section is one incredible talk that has two parts.

The first part of the talk comes in verses 17-27. It is a great report of all of Paul's missionary activities. What does Paul say that you would also like to be able to say by the end of your life?

The second part of the talk, in verses 28-38, contains practical advice to the members of the church. What parts of this counsel would increase the likelihood that you would have more experiences like verses 36-38?

Day 199, Acts 21:1-17

Paul takes time to meet with several of the saints as he travels to Jerusalem (:4, 7-8, 16-17). While traveling, do you take the time to meet and gather together with other saints?

The spirit often prepares us for that which is to come (:4, 9-13). When have you experienced this?

Paul was ready to be bound or to die for the gospel. We are not asked to do that, instead we will be asked to really live the gospel at home with our families and serve our neighbors. Will you answer these calls like Paul by saying "I am ready" (:13)?

Day 200, Acts 21:18-40

The Law of Moses was given to prepare people for the coming Messiah. After Christ came, these sacrifices were no longer needed. In verses 18-25, you will see that was difficult for the Jewish-Christians to give them up. We can hasten or hinder the work of the Lord by how we respond to change.

In verses 26-40 Paul is arrested at the Temple Mount because of a misunderstanding. The Jews believed that Paul took Gentiles into the unauthorized area on the Temple Mount. How often does misunderstanding lead to anger, hurt feelings, and miscommunication?

Day 201, Acts 22

As Paul begins a defense of his actions to the assembled crowd, he recounts his upbringing and history (:1-5). What elements of Paul's past made change and conversion unlikely. How can this help us as we look at the past of others and ourselves?

President Ezra Taft Benson gave the following caution when reading verses 6-21 "We must be careful, as we seek to become more and more godlike, that we do not become discouraged and lose hope. Becoming Christlike is a lifetime pursuit and very often involves growth and change that is slow, almost imperceptible. The scriptures record remarkable accounts of men whose lives changed dramatically, in an instant, as it were: Alma the Younger, Paul on the road to Damascus, Enos praying far into the night, King Lamoni. Such astonishing examples of the power to change even those steeped in sin give confidence that the Atonement can reach even those deepest in despair. But we must be cautious as we discuss these remarkable examples. Though they are real and powerful, they are the exception more than the rule. For every Paul, for every Enos, and for every King Lamoni, there are hundreds and thousands of people who find the process of repentance much more subtle, much more imperceptible. Day by day they move closer to the Lord, little realizing they are building a godlike life. They live quiet lives of goodness, service, and commitment. ... We must not lose hope. Hope is an anchor to the souls of men. Satan would have us cast away that anchor. In this way he can bring discouragement and surrender. But we must not lose hope. The Lord is pleased with every effort, even the tiny, daily ones in which we strive to be more like Him. Though we may see that we have far to go on the road to perfection, we must not give up hope" ("A Mighty Change of Heart," Ensign, Oct. 1989, 5).

What understanding does this quote bring?

After hearing Paul's testimony the group revolts, the chief wants him scourged, and Paul declares his Roman citizenship (:22-30).

Day 202, Acts 23:1-15

In verses 1-10 Paul is brought before a council composed of Pharisees and Sadducees. Paul uses each group's differences in beliefs to divide them. Look for what they disagreed about.

At some point our belief will come down to an acknowledgment or disassociation with angels, visions, dreams, and feelings (:9). Do you believe in these things? Have you experienced these things?

In the midst of people questioning the reality of Paul's vision, he receives another (:11). In this short one verse vision, what does the Lord say that could have brought encouragement to Paul or to us?

Day 203, Acts 23:16-35

In the last section there was a plot made to kill Paul. In this section we will see the discovery and exposure of the plot in verses 16-22, and then the creation of a counter plot to send Paul to Felix in verses 23-34.

"But do not thou yield unto them" (:21). Learning who to yield to and who not to yield to, are important decisions to make. Who do you choose to yield to?

What can we learn from these men who defended Paul's rights and freedoms even though they didn't agree with his beliefs?

Day 204, Acts 24

Notice all of the fake compliments and charges presented in verses (:1-9). In your opinion, why is an honest compliment more important than a fake one?

Verses 10-21 are Paul's defense of the charges against him. Watch for how he uses his defense as an opportunity to share his testimony. In what ways can you more often share your testimony without being an annoying nuisance?

What do you like, and what do you not like about the way that Felix treats Paul while he is in prison (:22-27)?

Day 205, Acts 25

Felix is replaced as Procurator by Festus after Jewish delegation complained formally about Felix in Rome. Watch how Festus tries to maneuver the political waters of respecting the Jews and their customs and yet remember that he faces toward Rome (:1-12). Which way do you face? Once I was asked "Which of these do you put first: your church calling, your work, or your family?" After a short discussion the wise answer was provided "If your answer is always the same then you are wrong." This doesn't mean that we love God or our families any less, but that we use the Holy Ghost to discern importance.

In verses 9-12 Paul rejects Festus' idea of returning to Jerusalem to be subject to Jewish law. Paul also bypasses Festus' Procurator judgment and makes an appeal to the Emperor, a right that all Roman citizens had.

Under Roman rule the Jews were allowed to maintain their own legal and political system (:13-27). Herod Agrippa II was the Jewish king and was the head of the delegation to Rome against Felix. Both Festus and Agrippa have relinquished authority over Paul's case, and yet they both desire to hear Paul speak for himself (:22). Curiosity leads us to inquiry, which leads us to learning. Paul's most powerful talk came because two men are curious. What will you learn today because you are curious?

Day 206, Acts 26

This is the third time we have heard Paul's conversion story. Is there a pivotal moment in your life that you frequently refer back to as a key to the rest of your life?

Paul frequently speaks about his former life (:1-11). How would you describe your former life, or your life before you really believed in Christ?

In verses 24-32 there is a great dialogue that follows Paul's speech. King Agrippa admits that Paul has almost persuaded him to become a Christian (:28). Has Paul persuaded you?

Day 207, Acts 27:1-26

Paul is being transferred to Rome. Notice how difficult this journey was in verses 1-11. Paul is a prophet, seer, and revelator and only warns when the course chosen is a dangerous one. Prophets warn us of things that if clung to would destroy us. What are some prophetic warnings that have protected you in the past?

The centurion believed the master and owner of the boat more than Paul, who doesn't have an expertise in sea travel, nor does he own the boat (:11). Without a testimony of prophets, I think all of us would make that same choice. What are some reasons why people may choose not to listen to prophets when they speak or give counsel today?

During a nasty storm and without hope of being saved, Paul said, "be of good cheer, for I believe in God" (:20, 25). How could that phrase help us when we find ourselves in difficult and nasty circumstances?

Day 208, Acts 27:27-44

In the last section, we saw how the centurion and others questioned Paul's counsel for various reasons. In today's section, look for places where people now have confidence in Paul's counsel.

What wrecks and recoveries have you had that have built your confidence in the council of prophets and apostles?

Day 209, Acts 28

What is your favorite detail in verses 1-10 that proves that Paul is a boss?

There is a group of saints that have traveled to meet up with Paul. Look for what this does for Paul in verse 15. How do you think our faith and courage can strengthen the apostles?

In Rome, Paul is put under a kind of house arrest. You would think that it would be difficult to preach the gospel while in prison, but look for how Paul does it and how effective it is in verses 16-31.

Day 210, Romans 1

The letter to the Romans appears after the book of Acts in the King James Version, because the epistles are positioned based on length and doctrinal significance, and not in a chronological order. Paul wrote to the members in Rome to prepare them for an upcoming visit and to correct false ideas. 10 of the 16 chapters deal with the relationship between the Law of Moses and the Christian gospel.

Paul is speaking to a group of saints that he had never met before. So he takes time to establish a relationship. In verses 1-17, look for what Paul says about himself, about the Roman saints, and about his purpose.

Paul is going to set up why we need a Savior in verses 18-32. He shows us the depravity of human nature in these verses. Somewhere in these verses, you will see that side of yourself that you are ashamed of. Yep, me too.

Day 211, Romans 3

Verses 1-8 are made easier by footnotes 1a, and 5a.

To solidify his argument that no mortal individual can be justified by obedience to the Law, Paul quotes several scriptures from the Old Testament in verses 9-20. If we are all failing, how can any one of us ever hope to be justified before God? It is not a matter of doing more, or enough.

In the book of Romans, Paul has made it clear that everyone is a sinner, and that the Law or obedience to commandments can't save us. Look in verses 21-31 for what Paul teaches that *can* save us.

Day 212, Romans 4

In chapter 3, Paul taught that we are able to stand before God because of faith and not because of our own works. Now Paul will use Abraham as an example of this. Look for how Abraham's faith justified him.

Notice footnotes 2a, and 16a.

Which phrase in verses 18-21 would you also like to have said of you?

Day 213, Romans 5

I invite you to read through verses 1-5 carefully a couple of times. Look for what else faith can bring into our lives.

If we are not careful, Paul's intense language in verses 6-21 may cause brain damage. He is teaching simple truths about the creation, the fall, and the atonement.

Why do you think that simple subjects can become difficult when we start to try to explain and understand them?

Day 214, Romans 6

In the last chapter we learned that there is sin because of the Fall and grace because of the Atonement. In this chapter Paul points out that because of sin and grace there is baptism. In verses 1-5 look for what you can learn about the symbolism of baptism.

Verses 6-23 is a wonderful discourse about the rewards of sin. What sin in your life do you wish would just die?

The idea of yielding is interesting in verses 13, 16, and 19. What will you yield your agency to today?

Day 215, Romans 7

How does Paul use the analogy of a wife whose husband has died to teach about the Law of Moses in relationship to the gospel of Christ?

In verses 5-14 Paul begins explaining how the commandments were intended for our salvation, improvement, and benefit. The commandments brought both sin and blessings the moment that they were given. Doesn't verse 15 echo how we have all felt about our own sins?

In verses 16-24 Paul will argue that there is a spirit and flesh side to all of us, and that this battle represents the human condition. According to verse 25, what is the solution to this dilemma?

Day 216, Romans 8:1-21

Paul continues with his discussion about the dual nature of spirit and flesh. In verses 1-13 look for what the results are of following each. Do you think it is easy to know which part of us is in charge in any given moment?

Verses 14-21 speak about the wonderful doctrine of spiritual adoption. When we accept Christ's gospel, we become more than just the spirit children of Heavenly Father, we now have bodies of spirit and flesh and we need all of that to be adopted. Thus, Christ becomes the Father of our resurrected and believing selves. Notice the promise made in verse 17, which clearly teaches the deification of those who have entered into an adoptive/covenant relationship with Jesus Christ.

Ab = Father. "Abba" = Daddy/Papa (:15). What does that say about the intimacy of this relationship?

Day 217, Romans 8:22-39

We frequently say routine checklist prayers that don't have much feeling. What do verses 26-27 suggest about how to know what we should be praying for?

Verse 28 is incredibly comforting, and I have found it to be true in my own life. If you are facing terrible hardships right now hold on and pray like the previous verses counseled.

Verses 29-34 only make sense if a person believes in a premortal life. The word "Predestination" in verses 29-39 doesn't mean destined or compelled, but appointed, or foreordained see footnotes 29c, and 30a.

In verses 35-39, what does Paul say could cause God to lose his love for us?

Day 218, Romans 9:1-15

In verses 1-3, Paul expresses his agony about the fact that many people who have sacred promises with God don't allow those covenants to really change them (:4-8). How can a person be of Israel without being Israel? What is the role of covenants in your life?

Verses 10-15 mentions several people who were elected to be of great service. What things do you think you were called or elected to do in your own life?

What do you think we are to make of the "hate" mentioned in verse 13, especially when in just the last chapter Paul mentioned that nothing can separate us from the love of God?

Day 219, Romans 9:16-33

In verses 18-23, Paul compares God to a potter making pots. What is the difference between making the pot versus filling the pot?

In verses 24-33, we have two groups/cups. The Jews were a cup filled with covenants and blessings. The Gentiles were a cup empty of covenants and blessings. Look for what each group does with their cup and its contents.

Day 220, Romans 10

Most of the arguments that religious people have with each other are about policies, practices, or traditions. The early Christians consisted of two major groups: Jewish Christians, who believed that adherence to the Law of Moses was essential, and the Gentile Christians, who believed that faith in Jesus Christ was essential. Look in verses 1-13 for how Paul corrects the argument about policy and practice by teaching correct doctrine. What policies or practices have you seen people fight over? What correct doctrines would have helped in those cases? When something bothers you, why would it be worth your time to determine if it is a doctrine, a policy, or a practice?

Paul has established that faith in Christ is essential for salvation. Look in verses 14-15 for how faith in Christ is developed. What role do families, scriptures, prophets, others, and you play in this process?

Why do you think Christ is still stretching forth his hand to those in need (:21)? How well do you stretch out your hand to others?

Day 221, Romans 11:1-18

There have been times that Israel has struggled to be faithful to God and the prophets. It is natural to wonder if God wants to cast his people away, but look at how Paul describes God's feelings about Israel in verses 1-10.

Grace can mean unmerited kindness, and also the enabling power. To be elected means to be called or chosen. To make that election sure, people must do what D&C 29:7 declares when it says "for mine elect hear my voice and harden not their hearts." How do these terms help you understand the previous verses?

In verses 11-18, Paul warns the Gentiles against being boastful about themselves accepting the gospel, while the Jews, chosen Israel, struggle to accept it. Why do you think this is a difficult challenge for people who have the gospel?

Day 222, Romans 11:19-38

In verses 19-32, Paul continues to warn those who have the gospel to not be too proud. He also teaches about the "goodness and severity of God" (:22). I believe that this quote will be of help in today's verses: "Our heavenly Father is more liberal in His views, and boundless in His mercies and blessings, than we are ready to believe or receive; and, at the same time, is more terrible to the workers of iniquity, more awful in the executions of His punishments, and more ready to detect every false way, than we are apt to suppose Him to be." (Teachings of the Prophet Joseph Smith, p. 257).

Which one do you feel more in your life: the goodness, or the severity of God?

This doctrine about God's goodness and severity leaves Paul with wonder and awe when he ponders it (:33-36).

Day 223, Romans 12

What do you think Paul means when he says to "present your bodies a living sacrifice, holy, acceptable unto God" (:1)?

How can changing your mind transform you (:2)?

After Paul has talked about the importance of our bodies and minds, he compares the church to a body with each individual, or member, making up the parts of the body. This is the reason that why we call people who belong to the Church members. What does Paul's counsel about how to be a good member in verses 5-21 teach us about individualism and unity?

Day 224, Romans 13

Paul now addresses one of the fundamental problems for those saints living in Rome. Who are they to show their allegiance to, God or the Roman republic? Look in verses 1-7 for what Paul says about what our relationship with government ought to be. Footnotes 1a, 1d, and 6a are helpful. These are some of the most abused and misunderstood passages from Paul. It is simple we render to the government what is theirs and to God what is His, and if the government tries to take what is God's then we don't have to oblige.

Paul now delivers several short messages about debt (:8), love of neighbor (:8-10), apathy (:11), and what to put on and take off (:12-14). Which one of these short little sermons would you hang on your bathroom mirror to remind you to do better?

Day 225, Romans 14

Paul attempts to address one of the most difficult things for any church, people taking offense because of each other's actions. In Rome many people offered meat offerings to their gods, and would then eat the meat. Because of this, many Christians didn't eat meat, but some still did. In verses 1-6, look for what was causing offense to some members. What types of things cause offense today?

In verses 7-12, Paul teaches the members of the Church that we are all connected, and that Christ is the ultimate judge to whom all will render an account one day.

It would be easy for Paul at this point to deliver a sermon about not judging, but instead he teaches an incredible idea in verses 13-23. If other members are losing their faith or being offended because someone is eating meat, what does Paul suggest that they do? What does this suggest about the type of love that we should have for each other? What about our politics, habits, dress, diet, language, mannerisms, or other things that sometimes cause people to stumble in their faith?

Day 226, Romans 15:1-13

After reading verses 1-7 what truth would you attach to each of the following words: weak, strong, please, patience, hope, one, and receive? When have you seen people fulfill the counsel in these verses?

To prove that Christ was sent to fulfill not only the promises made to the house of Israel, Paul quotes four scriptures in verses 8-12 (Psalm 18:19, Deuteronomy 32:43, Psalm 117:1, and Isaiah 11:1,10) that the Gentiles, nations not of Israel, would one day have the gospel. Because of this, look for what is promised in verse 13. Why do you think God chooses to let us feel those things instead of other feelings? Would you want to trade out any of those promises?

Day 227, Romans 15:14-33

Paul is beginning to say farewell to the Roman saints, and leaves them with a few bits of counsel. In verse 14, Paul tells these saints that they are good and knowledgeable enough to warn each other. Is it our responsibility to warn others, and how does a person do that without coming across as soap boxy?

Paul will use the word "minister" a couple of times in verses 16, 25, and 27. Look for what the word minister means in footnote 16a. Who do you know that is in need of ministering?

Speaking of his work among the Gentiles, Paul mentions that there were many mighty signs and wonders that happened by the power of the Holy

Ghost (:19). What signs and wonders could your own life add to the collection of spiritual manifestations?

Day 228, Romans 16

Paul greets, salutes, and commends 36 individuals in this chapter. How do you think that made these individuals feel? I invite you to send a kind e-mail, text, or make a phone call to let someone know that you love and care about them today.

Why might the counsel in verses 17-18 maybe even more valuable today than it was in Paul's day?

Day 229, 1Corinthians 1

Paul starts this epistle with an introduction of himself and the shared faith in Christ that all saints have (:1-9).

Perfect unity is always the saint's aim. Paul wastes no time in addressing the division and contention that the saints of Corinth are facing in verses 10-16. What resulted from these divisions? What can D&C 76:99-101 add to our understanding about the dangers of contention and disharmony?

How does Paul use the themes of wisdom, foolishness, and weakness to explain the gospel message and its messengers in verses 17-31? Are you weak and foolish enough to believe and proclaim the gospel?

Day 230, 1 Corinthians 2

There are strategies that enhance the likelihood that effective communication will take place. In today's section, Paul shares his methods for preaching the gospel to those who are not of the faith in verses 1-5, and for those who are in the faith in verses 6-16.

Just as Spanish can be foreign and indecipherable to one, so the language of the Spirit is to another (:11). How is a person able to determine their level of fluency in this language?

Verse 14 describes the feelings of those who do not hear the music of the gospel. Was there ever a time that you felt the same way? If so, what changed?

Day 231, 1 Corinthians 3

In verses 1-8 Paul uses the word "carnal" to mean worldly. Because of the self-imposed spiritual limits that the saints at Corinth have placed on themselves, Paul is only able to feed them with milk, and to plant the gospel, knowing that growth and increase will come from God. Are you and I living below our feeding and growth potential? Are we chewing the gospel and letting roots grow deep, or are we still being nursed along in shallow soil?

In verses 8-17 Christ is compared to a master builder, and we are His fellow laborers. Look for what we can withstand and what we can become when we are built on Christ's foundation.

Are you daily laboring to produce eternal things? Paul compares the wisdom of the world and how hard it works to produce temporary things to the wisdom of God, who seeks to give his saints "all things" (:21-22).

Day 232, 1 Corinthians 4

According to Paul, the greatest hindrance to preaching the gospel is disobedient missionaries (:1-2). Then, Paul warns us against judging others and worrying about them judging us in verses 3-5. Look for what Paul says Christ's judgment will do in verse 5.

Transferring the gospel to others and being able to receive it from others are both essential skills. Which one do you think you are better at?

A fulfillment of verses 9-13 could have been seen in the comment section of any newspaper that reported the passing of President Boyd K. Packer.

Paul feels for Corinth as a father does for his children, and will warn, love, and correct them to help them stay faithful (:14-21).

Day 233, 1 Corinthians 5

In today's section, Paul is adamant that a member of the Church in Corinth should be excommunicated. Look for what this member did, and the reasons Paul gives for why he should be excommunicated. In what ways could excommunication be a blessing?

In verses 9-11, Paul warns the saints about certain types of people not to keep company with. If you were God who would you put on your warning list?

Day 234, 1 Corinthians 6

In verses 1-8, Paul gets after the saints for taking each other to legal courts rather than working out their issues.

In verses 9-10, Paul lists things that would keep people from inheriting the kingdom of God. Then carefully read verse 11 and look for how it builds your faith.

The city of Corinth struggles with immorality. Look for Paul's reasons as to why a person should not commit sexual sin in verses 12-20. Which of Paul's reasons do you find personally compelling?

Day 235, 1 Corinthians 7:1-19

In the last chapter, Paul warned of sexual immorality. Verses 3-4 are about how intimacy is to be shared between a husband and a wife. Verse 5 contains a wonderful sermon about the ability of fasting to control sexual desire. Paul also added that if a person is unable to control that power they should marry.

One thing that can add difficulty in a marriage is if the couple doesn't share the same religious beliefs. In verses 10-19, you can discover Paul's counsel to the saints of Corinth who wondered if they should leave their spouses. How would you summarize Paul's teachings?

Day 236, 1 Corinthians 7:20-40

Living a life of slavery has been a reality for many of God's children. Paul gives counsel to those whose life is lived in unfavorable circumstances in verses 20-24. This is not a revolution of a social, or economic system, this is a revolution of an individual's heart. If you struggle finding satisfaction, how could these verses help?

Verses 25-40 often cause great confusion and hurt feelings, because Paul was answering a question about marriage that the Corinthians asked that is

81

not in this text. The question revolved around whether missionaries/ministers should be married before they perform their service. Make sure to check out verses 25, 35, and footnotes 26a, 29a, and 38a.

Day 237, 1 Corinthians 8

The saints of Corinth wanted to know if they could eat the meat that had been sacrificed to idols. Paul responded that his answer would provide knowledge, but that knowledge can make a person become puffed up. More important than knowledge about this question is charity. Charity for whom? Look for what charity had to do with eating meat.

What does verse 13 teach you about Paul's charity for his fellow believers?

To every God there is a pedigree, our Father in Heaven is no exception. In the midst of answering the meat question, Paul gives some of the best scriptures about the plurality of gods and our relationship to them (:5-6).

Day 238, 1 Corinthians 9

Paul will use several rhetorical questions in verses 1-13. Take your time as you read to answer these questions, in order, to understand what is being taught.

Paul is known for his missionary zeal. In verses 14-23, Paul shares with us several ideas about preaching the gospel. Which of these ideas do you feel could help you with your missionary efforts?

Verses 24-27 are incredible. How would you summarize what you learned from them?

Day 239, 1 Corinthians 10:1-15

Verses 1-15 give a brief review of Moses and the Children of Israel, accompanied with several lessons that Paul thinks that we should learn from them.

In the midst of all of these lessons, Paul delivers one particularly powerful verse about temptations (:13).

Day 240, 1 Corinthians 10:16-33

In verses 16-33, Paul compares the sacrament to the offerings made to idols. The sacrament is a weekly opportunity to consider what we are partaking of in our lives, for we are all offered many things throughout the week. As we pass the sacrament to others it gives us a chance to reflect on what we offered others to partake of this week.

Why and how do you think the sacrament produces greater unity among the saints?

Day 241, 1 Corinthians 11:1-16

The challenge of every teacher is to live and practice what they preach (:1). How well do the principles that you preach match your every day practices? Can we say what Paul said?

After addressing several questions in the last chapters, Paul now begins to correct and warn the saints of Corinth. Beginning with addressing a particular custom concerning women. In verse 5, notice what Paul does and doesn't have a problem with. In the eternal sense, it doesn't matter if a woman's head is covered or not when she prays or prophecies. In Paul's day it was viewed as irreverent for a woman to pray with her head not covered, because a woman's hair was considered to be highly erotic. Paul also warns that an uncovered head maybe mistaken for a shaved head, a sign of shame worn by women who were identified as an adulteress.

Some of the principles mentioned in today's section will appear sexist, but the government order that Paul is speaking of, only works when a man is totally subject to Christ, like Adam. Then, a woman like Eve could and would be subject to the man, who is now a man in Christ. Paul is completely aware that men and women need each other for exaltation (:11), but he also puts men in the position of presiding over the family, the principles for which are found in (D&C 121:41-46).

Day 242, 1 Corinthians 11:17-34

Today, Paul continues his corrections in verses 17-19. Why do you think it is important that when we gather with the saints, we seek unity rather than divisions and fractions?

83

Footnote 20a and the knowledge that the sacrament used to be a full meal will be helpful in understanding verses 20-26, and 33-34. Because the sacrament was a full meal, some came with more food than others, and some would come drunk, which could, in some cases, improve the talks.

Read verses 27-32 and the following quote:

"I suggest that perhaps some of us are ashamed to come to the sacrament table because we feel unworthy and are afraid lest we eat and drink of these sacred emblems to our own condemnation. And so we want every Latter-day Saint to come to the sacrament table because it is the place for self-investigation, for self-inspection, where we may learn to rectify our course and to make right our own lives, bringing ourselves into harmony with the teachings of the Church and with our brethren and sisters. It is the place where we become our own judges. There may be some instances where the elders of the Church could say, properly, to one who, in transgression, stretches forth his hands to partake of the emblems: 'You should not do this until you have made restitution;' but ordinarily we will be our own judges. If we are properly instructed, we know that it is not our privilege to partake of the emblems of the flesh and blood of the Lord in sin, in transgression, or having injured and holding feelings against our brethren and sisters. No man goes away from this Church and becomes an apostate in a week or in a month. It is a slow process. The one thing that would make for the safety of every man and woman would be to appear at the sacrament table every Sabbath day. We would not get very far away in one week—not so far away that, by the process of self-investigation, we could not rectify the wrongs we may have done. If we should refrain from partaking of the sacrament, condemned by ourselves as unworthy to receive these emblems, we could not endure that long, and we would soon, I am sure, have the spirit of repentance. The road to the sacrament table is the path of safety for Latter-day Saints." (Melvin J. Ballard, "The Sacramental Covenant" Delivered at a June Conference; printed in Bryant S. Hinckley, Sermons and Missionary Services of Melvin Joseph Ballard, Deseret Book Co., 1949, pp. 147–57).

Day 243, 1 Corinthians 12

Everyone has spiritual gifts, and they are enhanced and multiplied by the gift of the Holy Ghost accompanied by righteous desires. Read verses 1-11 and identify many of the spiritual gifts that exist. Do you have any of the gifts mentioned? To identify your gifts, consider your patriarchal blessing, as well as complements that your family, friends, and fellow saints give you.

Does Paul's discussion of the body parts in comparison the church in verses 12-31 make you feel more, or less important?

Some key verses regarding spiritual gifts, are 3, 7, 11, and 31.

Day 244, 1 Corinthians 13

Paul has just finished talking about spiritual gifts, he now brings up the greatest gift. In verses 1-3 look for what this gift is and what we are without it.

In verses 4-8, the qualities of this gift are more specifically named. In Moroni 7:47, there is an alternative name for this gift. Once you know that other name it is very interesting to read verses 4-8 again substituting this new name in place of the old one. What did you learn from doing this?

What difference does Paul say this gift will make in us one day (:9-13)?

Day 245, 1 Corinthians 14:1-25

Today Paul is going to compare the gift of tongues and prophecy. When are these gifts valuable and when are they not? Footnote 2a is helpful.

How can you use your gifts to edify, or lift up others instead of just yourself?

When have you been lifted up, or edified because of someone's wise use of their gift?

Day 246, 1 Corinthians 14:26-38

In verses 26-33, we can see the benefit of having several people use their spiritual gifts to edify or lift all. Think of all the gifts and talents that have been used in your ward in the last month. How have you benefited recently because of someone else's gifts?

There are hints that something is wrong with the text in verses 34-35. First, these verses are totally out of line with Paul's teachings in 1 Corinthians 11:5. Second, these passages seem to presuppose that women in Paul's congregations were completely silent. This is also at odds with what we

85

know (see Acts 18:2-3, 26; Rom 16:1-7; and Phil 4:2). Third, the JST footnote 34b, and 35a both change the word speak to rule. Paul would then be reminding the sisters to be subject to priesthood as the priesthood is subject to God. This is true for all members both male and female who are asked to follow priesthood leadership.

Day 247, 1 Corinthians 15:1-28

Which of the different sources that Paul uses to confirm the resurrection do you like the best in verses 1-11?

Some of the saints at Corinth are struggling to believe in the resurrection. What does Paul say would happen if there were no resurrection in verses 12-19?

What do verses 20-22 teach us about the connection between the Fall and the resurrection?

All people ever born will be resurrected. The only question left is, when? What do we learn about order of the resurrection from verses 23-28?

Day 248, 1 Corinthians 15:29-58

The Corinthian saints have struggled to understand the resurrection. To help them connect the simple doctrines of the gospel, Paul uses their experience performing baptism for the dead to increase their appreciation for the resurrection (:29). Baptism for the dead would be completely ridiculous is there was no life after, or resurrection from death. Work for the dead often produces many of our most spiritual and peaceful experiences. What value have these ordinances played in your own life?

If we were not eternal beings, If there was no resurrection then Paul's counsel would be verse 32. Since there is a resurrection he counsels us to do verses 33-34.

In verses 35-58, Paul continues to teach about the resurrection answering questions about what type of resurrected body a person receives because of faithfulness, how quickly, and what we should do because there will be a resurrection. Which teaching about the resurrection did you enjoy the most from this section?

Day 249, 1 Corinthians 16

In verses 1-4 Paul gives instruction for making a donation to help the saints of Jerusalem. What benefits have you received for paying, collecting, receiving, or managing fast offerings?

What final phrase of counsel do you love from verses 13-16? Check out footnotes 13d, and 15b.

Day 250, 2 Corinthians 1

As you read today's section, look for what promises Paul says that the gospel offers.

The Apostles are always doing so much for the members of the church. What does Paul teach us that we can do for them in verse 11? What does that mean for us with General Conference approaching?

Day 251, 2 Corinthians 2

In his last letter to the Corinthians, Paul got after them pretty good. In this letter he seeks to make sure that they know how deeply he cares for them, even when he corrects them. In today's section Paul will set an example of how to have an increase of love for someone after correcting them. What did you learn about the type of relationships saints should have?

When have you experienced what Paul is speaking about?

Was there any counsel that is particularly helpful at this time for you?

Day 252, 2 Corinthians 3

In verses 1-11 Paul compares the difference between the old covenant and the Law of Moses vs. the New covenant and the law of the gospel. Do we need laws in stone, or can we responded to the impressions of the heart? Do we need letter and scriptures detailing our actions, or can we yield to the whispering of spirit?

Christians and Jews both believe in the Old Testament, but Jews refer to it as the Hebrew Bible, because they do not believe that Jesus Christ was the promised Messiah, and are still waiting. Paul compares the inability to see

Jesus in the Old Testament to wearing a veil, and that only by turning and looking for the Lord will this veil be removed (:12-18). What Old Testament stories do you know of that contain powerful symbols of Christ?

The real question is, do you see stories and evidence of redemption and Atonement in your life and in the lives of those who surround you?

Day 253, 2 Corinthians 4

Those who have received the gospel now have a responsibility to help others receive it. In verses 1-7 Paul speaks about how we are to present the message, and also why some don't receive it.

Verses 8-18 can all be summarized by verse 17, and a quote from CS Lewis. "It is a serious thing to live in a society of possible gods and goddesses, to remember that the dullest and most uninteresting person you talk to may one day be a creature which, if you saw it now, you would be strongly tempted to worship, or else a horror and a corruption such as you now meet, if at all, only in a nightmare. All day long we are, in some degree, helping each other to one or other of these destinations. It is in the light of these overwhelming possibilities, it is with the awe and the circumspection proper to them, that we should conduct all our dealings with one another, all friendships, all loves, all play, all politics. There are no ordinary people. You have never talked to a mere mortal. Nations, cultures, arts, civilization—these are mortal, and their life is to ours as the life of a gnat. But it is immortals whom we joke with, work with, marry, snub, and exploit—immortal horrors or everlasting splendors." (The Weight of Glory, Preached originally as a sermon in the Church of St Mary the Virgin, Oxford, on June 8, 1942: published in THEOLOGY, November, 1941, and by the S.P.C.K, 1942, p.9)

Day 254, 2 Corinthians 5

Which verse in verses 1-11 do you think best describes the purpose of this life?

In what ways does Christ's death give your life more meaning (:15)?

Reconciliation means to return to harmony and unity between God and man (:18-21). When have you felt the distance narrow between you and God?

Day 255, 2 Corinthians 6

The doctrine in verse 2 is best explained by also studying Alma 34:31-34 in the Book of Mormon.

There are two great videos to go with verses 14, and 17.

To find the video for verse 14 you can do a search for "LDS equally yoked video." The words in the video are from Boyd K. Packer. I know that the end of the video is specifically about seminary and institute teachers, but the principle is applicable for all relationships. Odds are there is a relationship in your life right now that you could use greater unity in.

To find the video for verse 17 you can do a search for "LDS sanctify yourselves video." The words in the video are from Jeffrey R. Holland.

Day 256, 2 Corinthians 7

Notice how Paul and his companions were comforted in verse 6. Who have you comforted, or who has comforted you lately?

After studying verses 8-11, how would you describe the difference between guilt and godly sorrow?

Day 257, 2 Corinthians 8

Paul speaks of the generosity of the saints at Macedonia in giving to the poor (:1-5). Titus has been sent to the saints of Corinth for the same purpose (:6). In verses 7-15, Paul presents his invitation and advice for caring for the poor. What feeling is generated in you when you give to those in need?

In verses 16-23, the diligence, faithfulness, and trustworthiness of Titus and his companion are mentioned. There is no quicker way to lose your membership than to misuse the sacred funds of the church. Even anciently they handled the funds in pairs for protection.

I feel that verse 24 is best explained by a story told by Andrew Workman, an early Member of the Church: "I was at Joseph [Smith's] house. Several men were sitting on the fence. Joseph came out and spoke to us all. A man came and said that a poor brother who lived out some distance from town had had his house burned down the night before. Nearly all of the men said they felt sorry for the man. Joseph his hand in his pocket, took out five dollars and said: "I feel sorry for this brother to the amount of five dollars. How much do you all feel sorry?" (Juvenile Instructor, Oct. 15, 1892, 641.)

Day 258, 2 Corinthians 9

In verse 6, Paul uses an analogy from farming. If you plant a lot you can expect to harvest a lot. When have you experienced this principle in terms of giving to the poor?

Paul states it as a fact that "God loveth a cheerful giver" (:7). What are some of the advantages that come from wanting to give? What are some of the disadvantage that come from giving grudgingly?

Verses 8-15 contain some of the many blessing promised to those who seek to help the poor.

Day 259, 2 Corinthians 10

Because Paul is bold in his letters, he is often charged with not being in control of his words or emotions. In verses 4-7 look for what Paul says he is in control of. What advantages might come to a person who can control that?

How does a person learn or improve this control? Elder Bednar in his Face to Face meeting with the youth taught them to imagine that they have a container full of dark sand. With openings on each end only large enough for one grain of sand to fit through. When a white sand goes in it pushes a dark grain of sand out. While this doesn't change the contents of the container, if it is done enough then the desired change will come through time and practice.

Verses 8-18 deals with the topic of when and what to boast or not boast of.

Day 260, 2 Corinthians 11:1-15

Verse 4 has been used by many different people in an attempt to stop people from listing to missionaries. How do you think a careful reading of that verse can actually defuse this attack?

No one is getting rich by proclaiming the gospel or restored gospel of Jesus Christ (:7-9, 8a).

Verses 13-15 would be utterly terrifying if there was not a known key to protect use. This key is found in D&C 129:1-9, especially verse 8 which says that "you will not feel anything [both spiritually and physically]; you may therefore detect him."

Day 261, 2 Corinthians 11:16-33

Others boast of how good they are, Paul is going to boast of how much he has suffered. Check out his substantial list in verses 23-28.

How is suffering for Christ, because we love him, different than just enduring hard things?

This week, will you glory in and be grateful for your struggles because you believe rather than just complain about them?

Day 262, 2 Corinthians 12

As you read verses 1-4, look for what Paul teaches about visions and revelations without telling us specifically about them.

Despite the fact that Paul has had many visions and revelations he has also had a struggle that he refers to as "a thorn in the flesh" (:7). What does the Lord teach Paul about struggles and weakness in verses 8-10?

Paul admits he is concerned that the saints of Corinth will be struggling with verses 20-21. If Paul were to visit your ward or house, would he have need to be concerned?

Day 263, 2 Corinthians 13

The saints of Corinth have sought for proof that Paul is an apostle of Christ and now Paul invites these saints to prove that they are that they are in the faith (:1-5). Which proof is more important to you at this point in your life: proof that the gospel and its messengers are true, or proof that you are true to the gospel?

What do you think verse 8 means?

Paul is aware that his words can cause edification or destruction (:10). Will you build or destroy with your words today?

Day 264, Galatians 1

The saints of Galatia are struggling to remain faithful to the gospel that was preached to them by Paul (:6). The letter to the Galatians is to challenge and remind them that Jesus Christ and his gospel are the way to salvation, and not a mixture with the Law of Moses (:7-9).

What can we learn about gaining our own testimony from Paul's example in verses 11-12?

As you read verses 13-23 consider what ways Paul's past and conversion have become a benefit for the gospel.

Day 265, Galatians 2

In addition to preaching the gospel, what else was Paul told to pay special attention to in verse 10?

As part of the Law of Moses, the Jews would not eat meals with Gentiles. This law has been done away with and the gospel is being preached to the Gentiles. Peter is corrected by Paul when Peter separates himself from eating with the Gentiles when other Jews show up. Does it damage or strengthen your faith to see a prophet make a mistake and then receive correction from a fellow Apostle?

Verses 14-21 are not the first nor will it be the last time we read Paul making an argument that laws, and commandments are not sufficient to save us, we need a savior. Why do you think it is good for us to be reminded of the important and indispensable role of Christ in our salvation?

Day 266, Galatians 3

How does Paul feel about the Galatians turning to the Laws of Moses to save them rather than Christ (:1-4)?

To prove that a person can be saved without the Law of Moses, Paul makes his case by using the life of Abraham (:6-29). Which piece of evidence did you find most compelling?

In verses 23-25 we find an incredible summary and conclusion to the purpose of the Law. What was its purpose?

Day 267, Galatians 4

What is the difference between being a son or daughter of God and being a servant (:1-7)? How does a servant become a son or a daughter?

Paul describes his efforts to teach, and to now reteach, the Galatians as a labor comparable to giving birth, or at least rebirth. All of this teaching will be of no worth unless "Christ is formed in" them (:19). Spiritual birth happens as people start to think, feel, and act more like Christ. What can you do to help yourself, your family, and others have this kind of experience and not just go to Church?

Abraham's two sons are an analogy of the Law of Moses and the promise of Christ (:21-31).

Day 268, Galatians 5

Paul delivers so many great one-liners in this chapter. I invite you to read it carefully and find one that is significant to you.

Youth are often confused about what the spirit feels like, and are unsure if they have ever felt it. In verses 16-26 Paul not only teaches about the ways the spirit can feel, he also addresses the feelings of the flesh. These are some of the best verses in scripture for helping people learn about how the spirit feels when it communicates with them.

Day 269, Galatians 6

Who do you know that needs to be restored to faith, or from fault? What do you think Paul means when he counsels us to do this in a spirit of meekness?

We all get tired, we all get worn out, we all get churched, and we all need the advice of verse 9 sometimes. I know that I do. When we have those times or days that are particularly demanding and at the same time feel less than successful, it is helpful to remember that no righteous effort is ever wasted.

I love how practical verse 10 is in its approach to helping others, "As we have therefore opportunity." Watch for opportunities to serve others tomorrow and this week, but don't become overwhelmed.

Day 270, Ephesians 1

Paul's greetings are always rich with doctrine about Heavenly Father and Jesus Christ. This introduction also contains the remarkable truth that we were "predestined" or pre-anointed with the responsibility to share this gospel with our brothers and sisters who don't have it yet. Which of the doctrines mentioned in the introductory verses 1-9 did you notice this time?

Verses 10-13 deal with the promised gathering in the dispensation of the fullness of times. All who have heard the gospel and trusted in Christ and believed (:13), as it was preached by those who were selected in the premortal life (:11), will receive the Holy Ghost which seals upon an individual the promise that if they continue to live their life in this way they will inherit exaltation (:13-14).

If you ever wanted to know what an Apostle might say in a prayer offered for the saints there is a sample found in verses 15-23. Look for what he prays for us to receive and what he wants us to know about Christ.

Day 271, Ephesians 2

In today's section Paul switches back and forth from describing our former life of sin before conversion and the life of a saint afterwards. Which verse do you think best describes each of these lives?

When was a time when you felt that the wall partitioning us from God had been broken down?

What do verses 19-22 teach you about how God builds everything in his kingdom?

Day 272, Ephesians 3

"The prisoner of Jesus Christ" (:1). This epistle marks the beginning of the prison letters that Paul wrote while he was a prisoner in Rome.

The great "mystery" mentioned in verses 2-13 is that God's plan to save his children always included a way for the Gentiles to become "fellow heirs" with the Jews and the House of Israel (:6). Why do you think it is so important to know that God desires the salvation of all of his children?

After a lengthy meditation, Paul continues his prayer for the Ephesian saints in verses 14-21. Look for what he prays for, and ask yourself if you ever pray to receive those things?

Day 273, Ephesians 4

In verses 1-6 look for what the saints are to be united in.

Verses 11-16 are perfect for times when General Conference is approaching, look for all of the reasons that the Lord has given us prophets, apostles, and teachers. Notice how long we will need these prophets, apostles, and teachers in verse 13. Which of the reasons given that we have prophets and apostles do you find yourself most grateful for?

Of all the things that Paul counsels us to "put on" and "put off" in verses 22-32 which ones do you think would most improve your life? Make sure you check out footnote 26a.

Day 274, Ephesians 5:1-16

What do verses 4, and 6 teach you about communication?

I love the idea that Paul doesn't want to speak about any of the things done in secret (:11-12), and yet he knows that the purpose of light is to manifest and expose them so that Christ can change and heal them (:13-14). The best thing for dark, nasty, secret things is to be thrown into the burning light of Christ. All of the dark things mentioned in verses 3-6 can be healed. I invite you that if there is something that you are hiding in the dark, to bring it out into the light and let it be consumed. I know that the shame will turn into peace quicker than you think. For that is what it means to be a "child of light," to be one who has come out from darkness (:8).

Day 275, Ephesians 5:17-33

One of the great blessings of serving in primary is the fulfillment of verse 19. What difference do those simple songs make in the way that you think, feel, and act throughout the day?

We receive a commandment in verse 20, but the promise for keeping it is found in D&C 78:19. Why do you think those promises are associated with that commandment?

Eternal marriage is the most important ordinance in LDS theology. Marriage has the power to turn couples into Gods, Angels, or Devils, and to make home a heaven or hell. How does Paul use the relationship between Christ and the Church to teach men and women about marriage in verses 21-33?

Day 276, Ephesians 6

In verses 1-9, Paul gives counsel to children, parents, servants and their masters. Look for what his advice is, and consider if you think his counsel still works if we change servant to employee and master to boss.

In verses 10-18, Paul turns his counsel to the brethren and we can add sisters of the church, that they should put on the "whole armor of God" (:11, 13). As you read you can consider and ponder about why each piece is important. Then prayerfully ask "what do I need to start, or stop doing to more fully put on the armor of God"?

Day 277, Philippians 1

This is the happiest of all of Paul's epistles, full of good counsel and confidence, it is also sent from prison.

Paul is very complementary of the saints at Philippi. Read verses 2-11 and look for a verse that you wish the same could be said of you.

How does Paul suggest that his time in prison and potential death are being used by the Lord to further the progress and preaching of the gospel in verses 12-26?

Day 278, Philippians 2

If there are any of the results of verse 1, then it is the result of the saints obtaining the attributes and desires mentioned in verses 2-4, and 6-8. Which means they have obtained the mind of Christ (:5). In what way can your adoption of these attributes help you think more like Christ?

Because of how well Christ accomplished his tasks, God the Father has declared the blessings of verses 9-11 to be fulfilled. Notice the word "every" in verses 9-11. This will not be the result of force but of willful adoration and respect for what He accomplished. The question is when will you and I make such declarations?

Because of the coming acknowledgement by all that Jesus is Lord, we are to do verses 12-16.

In verses 17-30, Paul recommends Timotheus and gives an explanation of Epaphroditus.

Day 279, Philippians 3

In verses 2-11 Paul warns people to beware of relying on the strength of their own flesh. Look in verses 7-9 for what Paul says everything else is when compared to the knowledge of Christ? Why do you agree or disagree with Paul?

In the Apostle Paul admission that he has not obtained perfection, what counsel does he provide about how to continue to grow in verses 12-16? Does this sound like push button salvation, or something a little harder?

There are always examples to follow. Who are the examples mentioned in verses 17-21, and where do they lead?

Day 280, Philippians 4

Article of Faith 13 is based on verse 8. What does it teach you about what truths Christianity embraces? What things come to your mind when you read this verse?

In addition to the redemptive power of the atonement, there is also the enabling power of grace that does just what verse 13 proclaims. Do you really believe that this power is available? If so, what will you ask to be strengthened in today?

Which of the following do you think contains the best mini lesson, verses 4, 5, 6-7 & 6a, or 11-12?

Day 281, Colossians 1

The saints at Colossae have been attacked with a wide variety of beliefs about who and what Jesus Christ is. There has always been confusion about both who and what Christ is. Here are what several religions believe about him.

Christian: most believe in the trinity. Divisions on Christ being divine or human are some of the major Christological positions.

Jehovah's Witnesses: Jesus is God's son or Jehovah's son. Michael was the archangel. Jesus was Man not a god, a spokesman for God and killed on a single stake not a cross.

Islam: Believes that Jesus is a prophet. That He was born from a virgin birth. Performed miracles, but was not crucified. They believe that He will come back in the last days to destroy Islam's enemies. Then He will die.

Judaism: They do not believe that He is the Messiah because, they feel He didn't meet the qualifications. They believe Jesus is a stumbling block who makes the world err. Anyone who claims salvation is in Jesus is not a Jew.

Hindu: Believe that Jesus was born of virgin. That He was a Brahmin within two births, and sent to preach of God. That He was a beloved son of Krishna, and a incarnation of Elisha, Elijah, or one of the Gods. Gandhi considered Jesus to be one of his main teachers and inspirations.

Buddhist: Jesus was one who dedicated his life to the welfare of human beings.

New Age: There are a variety of views, but most believe that Christhood, which is one of the steps of enlightenment, can be obtained by all people. He is called "Jesus the Master".

Deist: God doesn't interfere with the affairs of man. Jesus was a great moral and ethical teacher, but not the son of God.

Search verses 12-23 for words or phrases that Paul uses to teach about Christ. In what ways can you see that Paul's teachings are different from those above?

Day 282, Colossians 2

Yesterday Paul shared a powerful testimony regarding the Savior. Which of the following words do you think best describes his testimony: "rooted", "built up", "stablished", or "abounding" (:7)? Which of those words do you want to be used when describing your testimony of Christ?

This second chapter is given to help us understand what builds up, roots, establishes, and causes testimonies to abound. It also warns us against things that destroy and decompose testimony. Look for what you can learn about the building or breaking of a testimony.

Day 283, Colossians 3

Chapter 1 was about Paul's testimony, chapter 2 was about what we can do to build or break our own testimony. Chapter 3 is about how a testimony of the truth should stir us to action and a Christ like life. We will then be "risen with Christ," "setting our affections on things above," becoming "dead" to sin, we will be "hid" in Christ, "appearing like him in glory" (:1-4).

Think about the reasons why and how often you change your clothes. Paul invites us to do the same with actions. As you read verses 5-17 you may want to make a list of the different things that Paul counsels us to "mortifying" or "put off," and what we should "put on."

In verses 18-25, wives, husbands, children, fathers, and servants receive counsel. Which counsel do you like the best?

Day 284, Colossians 4

How would you rewrite verses 3-4 and 5-6 in your own words?

Who is a distant saint that you would wish to express your love and respect for (:7-15)?

Verse 16 makes mention of an "epistle from Laodicea." If you follow footnote 16a, it will take you to a very interesting Topical Guide page which will show you all of the scriptures that are mentioned in the Bible but that we don't have.

Day 285, 1 Thessalonians 1

Often new converts find it difficult to remain active, but not these saints. Look in verses 5-10 for what you think is the most impressive way that the saints of Thessalonica showed their faith.

True or false, there is much less of a need to preach the gospel if we live the gospel.

What is so incredible about the word "wait" in verse 10?

Day 286, 1 Thessalonians 2

In this chapter, Paul describes his missionary service and gives an incredible amount of detail about how to be a true missionary/preacher/teacher. Search verses 1-13, and 17-20 for principles on how to be a truly great missionary/preacher/teacher.

Day 287, 1 Thessalonians 3

The most difficult and heartrending thing about proclaiming the gospel is the poor retention percentage of those who are newly converted. Paul has such fear for the new saints of Thessalonica. In verses 1-13, look for what Paul did so that his new converts didn't fall away.

Was there anything that you saw that you could do to help prevent the falling away of your friends and family?

What does verses 12-13 teach you about the reasons for the atonement?

Day 288, 1 Thessalonians 4

Being a Christian is not just about having a good relationship with God and Christ, it is also about treating others well. Thus, Paul gives counsel in verses 1-12 about how to be holy toward others.

Verses 13-18 are about a very specific doctrine regarding both living and dead saints at the time of the 2nd coming. Each of these cross references and footnotes will add additional meaning to what you learned 15a, 17a, D&C 45:44-46, and D&C 88:96-97.

Paul spoke these words to supply comfort, according to verse 18. How does this knowledge comfort you?

Day 289, 1 Thessalonians 5

In verses 2-3, Paul uses the images of a thief and childbirth to describe the second coming. What is the difference between how people prepare for childbirth versus a thief?

Which image do you think will best describe your experience with the second coming?

In verses 8-26, Paul gives us counsel on what we can do to prepare. What bit of advice seemed as though it were written to help you today?

Day 290, 2 Thessalonians 1

In this follow up letter, Paul claims that saints can receive and send a token or sign to God by how they use the concepts of faith, charity, patience, and endurance (:5). Read verses 3-4 and look for what must we do with each of those ideas.

As you read verses 6-9, you may have the question "Why will God destroy the wicked at his coming?" What insight does 1 Nephi 22:14-17 give you as to why he will destroy the wicked?

Day 291, 2 Thessalonians 2

The reason that Paul had to write a second letter is because the Thessalonian saints got so excited about the second coming mentioned in the first letter that many of them stopped working and planting crops because they felt it was going to happen that soon. In verses 1-3, two signs are pointed out that must happen before the second coming.

Some have mentioned that the "man of sin" in verse 3 is a false prophet or different organizations, but verses 4-9, and 7a make it clear that this is the Devil, and his work being exposed.

Because of apostasy and the temptations of the Devil, some will fall away or not believe (:10-12). What phrase does Paul say in verses 13-17 that encourages you to continue to choose faith and belief?

Day 292, 2 Thessalonians 3

Which set of verses do you like better: Paul's pleading for the saints' prayers in verses 1-2, or his expression of faith and confidence in verses 3-5?

What are the principles of work and welfare that are taught in verses 7-13?

Verses 6, and 14-15, may seem harsh at first, but they are counsel to church leaders about excommunication, and not to individual members. Notice the cross references in Alma 1:21-24, and Alma 5:56-57. How would you summarize what is being taught?

Day 293, 1 Timothy 1

This is the beginning of the pastoral, or letters to ministers. Look in verses 3-7, and 17-20, for what a minister/leader is supposed to teach and ensure is taught, and what they are not to teach.

What is the purpose of law according verses 8-10?

Paul's personal conversion story continues to be a source of learning for him. Search for what additional principles he has learned that are mentioned in verses 11-16.

Day 294, 1 Timothy 2

In verses 1-3 and 8, who does Paul mention that we should pray for? Are these people that are frequently included in your prayers?

I love the straightforwardness of verses 3-4. In what ways have you felt the Lord's desire to save you?

The counsel given in verses 9-10 is about "modest apparel". Modest in cost and style. When it comes to image there is a principle that is helpful: don't let our desire to increase our individual identity create a loss of our eternal identity.

It is clear that Paul had a limited understanding in verses 11-15 and could have benefitted greatly from 2 Nephi 2:22-25, D&C 29:39, and Moses 5:10-11. Paul apparently believed that Mother Eve overstepped her bounds, which is what transgression means, when she made a decision that affected Adam as well.

Day 295, 1 Timothy 3

Verses 1-7 describe the qualities that a bishop "must" have (:2). How do you think bishops feel when they read this list?

Verses 8-13 mention the qualities that a deacon "must" have (:8). It is worth noting that those ordained to the office of deacon were not always twelve years of age, but mostly grown men.

Being ordained to a priesthood office should be a challenging and elevating experience. When have you seen a man become a better man because he rose to the level of his ordination?

What connections do you see between priesthood power and the way that a priesthood holder is to treat his family members?

Day 296, 1 Timothy 4

In verses 1-9, look for what the Spirit warned Paul about the "latter times" (:1). Notice that some of these things are bad, and that some are good, and that if taken to extremes they keep us from doing what is most important. How well do you think you heed the warning from the Spirit in these verses?

In some way we are all teachers of the gospel. Carefully consider what each verse in 10-16 counsels teachers to do. What verse inspires you to do something about how you prepare, or teach the gospel?

Day 297, 1 Timothy 5

What experiences have you had that prove that respecting and learning from the elderly is a good gospel principle (:1-3)?

Couched in a discussion about how to take care of widows, is some of the best principles on welfare in all of scripture. Carefully read verses 4-16 and look for what you can learn about administering welfare. How would you summarize what you have learned?

Of the counsel given to the leaders of the Church in verses 17-25, which do you think is timeless? Notice footnote 22a, I think it is interesting.

Day 298, 1 Timothy 6

Why do you think Paul warns us about the type of people described in verses 3-5, and 20-21?

What do you believe are the three most important principles that we can learn about stuff and money from verses 6-12, and 17-19?

In verses 13-16, Paul reminded Timothy who his "charge" really comes from, and who he is responsible to. Why has it been important for you to remember that this is Christ's church and gospel?

Day 299, 2 Timothy 1

Any time we attempt to preach or teach the gospel, there is an opportunity for tremendous joy and/or disappointment. Watch for both as you read this chapter.

What does Paul say about the role that the Holy Ghost is to play in this process (:6-7, 13-14)?

I love the phrase that Jesus Christ "hath abolished death" (:10). What other things has Jesus abolished from your life?

Day 300, 2 Timothy 2

Paul draws on soldiers, a competitor, and a farmer to teach disciples some lessons (:3-4, 5, 5a, 6). What are we to learn from each of these?

Look at all of the "if" statements and their accompanying promises in verses 11-13.

In verses 15-26, Paul gives counsel that he has given us before. As you read it this time, look for a word or phrase that stirs you.

Day 301, 2 Timothy 3

In verses 1-9 look for the conditions that Paul said would exist in the last days. How accurate do you feel he is in describing our time?

In verse 13, Paul makes a statement letting us know that things are not going to be getting better. This chapter describes the ever increasing problems that we do and will face in the last days, but it also provides the solution. Read verses 14-17 to discover how to protect yourself and your loved ones. These verses are one of the major reasons that I decided to do Study Daily. In what ways have you felt the truthfulness of Paul's words and promises in your own life?

Day 302, 2 Timothy 4

Paul gives to Timothy his final "charge" to carry out before God and Christ in verse 1. Read verses 2-5 and see if you can summarize in one sentence what he was charged to do.

Most scholars believe that this is the last epistle and chapter that Paul wrote before his death. In verses 6-8, look for how Paul approached his coming death. What would it take for you to feel the same confidence that he had?

In what will become a dying request, Paul asks for a visit, a cloak, some books, "but especially the parchments" that the scriptures are written upon (:13). Does the word of the Lord play that same comforting role in your life? Can you become prepared for the day to come, the struggles ahead, and even death, by immersing yourself in the scriptures?

Day 303, Titus 1

In verse 2, Paul gives us a hint of his knowledge about the premortal life and the promises that were made to us there.

Titus has been left on Crete to set up the Church by finding leaders. In verses 5-9, Titus is given instruction about the type of qualities that leaders should have. As you read, consider how well you are doing at developing these skills and attributes so that the Lord can use you to bless the lives of others.

Just as there are qualities in leaders that build the Church, there are also qualities that would attempt to destroy the Church and belief. Look for what Titus is warned to correct in verses 10-16. Look at each quality and consider why it needs correcting.

Day 304, Titus 2

In today's section, Paul gives counsel to the aged men and women, young women and men, and servants. Which advice do you think is still relevant and thus timeless? Is there anything that is said to one group that wouldn't be useful to another group?

Who do you think of when you read of each of these different groups and ages?

Day 305, Titus 3

How accurately do verses 3-7 convey your own gospel story?

How would you summarize verses 3-7 into a single sentence? When you are done, you will know what the faithful saying mentioned in verses 8 is.

Have you ever seen any of the things that Paul warns us against in verse 9 destroy or distract a talk, lesson, or visit?

Day 306, Philemon

"This epistle is a private letter about Onesimus, a slave who had robbed his master, Philemon, and run away to Rome. [While in Rome Onesimus is converted to the gospel by Paul]. Paul sent him back to his master at Colosse in company with Tychicus the bearer of the epistle to the Colossians. Paul asks that Onesimus be forgiven and received back as a fellow Christian." (Bible Dictionary: "Pauline Epistles")

In verses 9-22, look for how Paul is asking for Philemon to change his relationship with Onesimus. Here we are only getting half of the conversation. Can you imagine what kind of talk must have happened between Paul and Onesimus about him returning to the life of slavery? Though not seen in these lines, Paul also was asking Onesimus to change his relationship to Philemon. Both of these men could have produced lists of wrongs done to them, and complained of hurt feelings.

Who is someone in your life that your relationship with needs to change for the better? The fundamental purpose of the atonement of Christ is to restore, rebuild, reestablish, reunite, rekindle, and exalt all relationships. What relationship do you need the atonement and its healing power to be placed on?

Day 307, Hebrews 1

"None of the books in the New Testament, the Gospels included, are more Christ centered than Paul's epistle to the Hebrews." (Joseph Fielding McConkie, "Jesus Christ, Symbolism, and Salvation," in Robert L. Millet, Studies in Scripture: Volume 6, Acts to Revelation [1987], 192).

Look for a couple of distinctive things that you learn about Christ from verses 1-3.

The message of chapter 1 is clear, Jesus Christ is greater than Angels. What are some of the reasons given for this?

Day 308, Hebrews 2

What do verses 1-4 warn us about drifting away from Christ's prophets and apostles? Why do you think people are more prone to slip and drift, than they are to rejection and fall?

Carefully read verses 9-18 and look for why it was necessary that Christ had to suffer, be tempted, and have a mortal life. Which verse do you think best described why? Have you felt the reality of those explanations in your own life?

Day 309, Hebrews 3

Moses is revered as a great prophet, maybe even the greatest. In verses 1-6 it is explained why Christ is greater than Moses.

In verses 7-19 we are told what the children did that caused them to wander for forty years in the wilderness, and also how we can prevent wandering in our own lives. What did you learn about the importance of "today"?

Day 310, Hebrews 4

In verses 1-11, what do we learn about the rest of the Lord, and about who will enter it, and who will not? Check out footnotes 3a, 5a, and 6a.

I love the description of the word of the God in verse 12. When would you describe a time in your life when you felt that the word of God was doing some of those things mentioned in this verse?

How can we approach the throne of God boldly and expect to receive grace and mercy if the word of God so clearly divides and reveals our true intentions (:16, 12-13)? What did you learn from verses 14-15, and how does it increase your feelings of appreciation?

Day 311, Hebrews 5

What do verses 1-4 teach us about the priesthood and about men who are ordained to it?

Verses 5-10 are incredible. What do they teach us about Christ and his ordination to the priesthood?

It has been over 10 years since the Jerusalem Conference where it was decided that Gentiles didn't have to accept the Law of Moses before becoming Christians (Acts 15). Since then, the Jewish saints have struggled to give up certain aspects of the Law of Moses and don't accept those who haven't accepted the Law. The book of Hebrews was written to this group, and verses 11-14 call them to repentance and demand of them to be more.

Day 312, Hebrews 6

Sometimes people are confused by the language of verse 1 about "leaving the principles and doctrine of Christ." It becomes clear when we look at footnotes 1a, the context of verses 1-3, and 2 Nephi 31:17-21. The goal of the doctrine of Christ is to move us toward eternal life and perfection through Christ.

Verses 4-9 speak of the impossibility of redeeming those who become Sons of Perdition. This is not because the atonement doesn't work, it is because those who become this choose to never repent, for if they did they would not be Perdition (:6). These are they who would have to be willing to crucify Christ knowing fully who he was (:6). Exaltation is for those who choose to become like the Father and the Son. Outer Darkness is for those who choose to become like the devil. That's hard to do.

Verses 10-20 contain the word "promise(s)" four times. These are the promises that God made through an oath that if he broke would tear His god hood from Him, and rip His power and authority away. In these verses look for all of the little things that are mentioned about who receives these promises and what kind of hope that brings. Are you doing the things to obtain these promises? Do you feel that kind of hope?

Day 313, Hebrews 7

Verses 1-11 teach us about the superiority of the Melchizedek priesthood over the Aaronic, it also mentions several cool things about Melchizedek. Then, verses 11-22 teach us the superiority of Christ's atonement compared to the Law of Carnal Commandments, or the Law of Moses. Are Jesus Christ and His gospel really superior to other philosophies, ideas, and beliefs in what they can do for you?

In case you're not sure, look at what the book of Hebrews claims about Christ in verses 25-28. Do you have a favorite little line about him from those verses?

Day 314, Hebrews 8

The tabernacle, the temple, the sacrifices, the priests, and the high priests are all the "example and shadow of heavenly things" (:5). The sum of it all pointing to Christ (:1-5, 4a).

Hundreds of years earlier the prophet Jeremiah prophesied that the God of Israel would establish a new covenant with His people (Jeremiah 31:31-34). This prophecy is declared fulfilled in the 8th chapter of Hebrews by the coming of Christ. Search for what your favorite promise is from verses 6-13.

Day 315, Hebrews 9

For a greater understanding of verses 6-28, see "Fasts" in the Bible Dictionary, paragraphs 3-4.

One of my favorite titles for Christ is found in verse 11, a "high priest of good things to come." Elder Jeffrey R. Holland has also given an incredible talk by this same title that would be valuable to look at ("An High Priest of Good Things to Come," Ensign, Nov. 1999).

What good things do you believe have come into your life because of Jesus Christ?

Day 316, Hebrews 10:1-18

On their own, neither sacrifice nor sacrament can save us and provide a remission of sins. These ordinances are "shadows" and done in "remembrance" of the real saving sacrifice performed by Christ (:1, 3). In today's section you will see the difference between animal sacrifice and the sacrifice of Jesus Christ.

If sacrifices and sacrament don't save us, then why are they important? Because when these things are done with the shadow or remembrance of Christ, the Holy Ghost can instill the laws and commandments into our hearts and minds (:15-16). The reception of the Holy Ghost is also the promise that our past sins will not be remembered nor mentioned by God (:17-18).

Here are a couple of other helpful references (Alma 34:8-17, Moses 5:4-11).

Day 317, Hebrews 10:19-39

The boldness of Jesus Christ's mediation as our high priest is so incredible that it allows us to do several things with greater confidence. Look for the phrase "let us" in verses 19-25 to discover some of these things.

Just as Christ offered more mercy than the Law of Moses, he also delivers greater justice. Verses 26-31 contain a serious and sober warning to those who know of the value of Christ's blood, yet treat it poorly.

As doubt, darkness, and discouragement come to all, there are words and phrases in verses 32-39 that will help provide the confidence, illumination, pleasure that we need. Which phrase captured you?

Day 318, Hebrews 11:1-19

This whole chapter is about faith. What are the great lessons you learn about faith from verses 1, and 6?

In today's section you will find many stories about people in the Bible who did remarkable things "by/through faith." Which of these stories is your favorite demonstration of faith? What will you do by/through faith today?

Day 319, Hebrews 11:20-40

Today, like yesterday, will be filled with many examples of people doing and enduring incredible things by, and through, faith. What will you do by/through faith today?

What do verses 23-26 teach you about sin and righteousness?

Footnote 40a is a help to us.

Day 320, Hebrews 12

We have just spent two days looking at great examples of people of faith who worked many miracles. What are we to learn from "so great a cloud of witnesses?" Look what verses 1-4 suggest.

Correction, chastening, and disciplined are words that can be hard to endure when they become reality. Carefully, and I mean carefully, read verses 5-11 and look for what our correct viewpoint should be regarding correction, chastening, and discipline.

Our situation of approaching the throne of God is compared to ancient Israel approaching Mount Sinai (:18-29). We can only hope to be allowed into the divine presence if we forsake sin (:1), patiently trudge along, look to Christ (:2), take correction (:5-11), and do verses 12-17. Don't be afraid of this burning and consuming fire that is the Lord. He is only removing those things that shake, and what will be left will be unmovable, unshakable, burned and not consumed (:26-29). We will be burning bushes in the presence of God.

Day 321, Hebrews 13

What is your favorite bit of closing counsel: the smattering of truths in verses 1-6, the importance of Christ in verses 8-16, or the need to support and sustain leaders in verses 7, 17-19, and 24?

Day 322, James 1

The epistle of James is not heavy on doctrine, unlike the writings of the apostle Paul. Instead, James is a book about practical living of the gospel of Christ. This James is believed to be the son of Joseph and Mary, half-brother to Jesus (Matthew 13:55).

Because of how good James is at making the gospel practical, you will get several short sermon type verses that are incredibly applicable. As you read, look for some principle that would have made yesterday easier if you had lived it.

If the measure of religion is verse 27, how good are you at being religious? What will you do to be more religious this week?

Day 323, James 2

In verses 1-9, James discourages favoritism to those who are wealthy over the poor. Learning to care about everyone regardless of class or merit, is at the root of developing Christ like love and compassion.

As we have read much of the New Testament, we have seen the struggle between the balance of faith and works. In verses 14-26 James delivers what maybe the best doctrinal explanation of the relationship between, and need for faith and works.

What work will you do today to show your faith?

Day 324, James 3

We have all put our foot in our mouth and said things that we are not proud of. James now calls for us to develop mastery of our speech, knowing that in attempting we will be held more accountable (:1a). What does this chapter teach you about controlling the tongue and heart?

Which of the analogies used by James do you think best describes the difficulty of controlling our mouths and words?

What subjects, people, or words do you need to take more caution with today as you speak?

Have you ever made controlling your speech a matter of prayer?

How would learning to master your tongue help you in all of your relationships with others?

Day 325, James 4

James continues with practical advice and application of the gospel. I would like to highlight just a few of them. How might a lust for pleasures, gratification, and passions lead to an increase of war, fighting, and arguing (:1, 1a)? What does this say about how to obtain peace?

Our prayers need direction from the Holy Ghost through thoughts and feelings so that we can avoid verse 3. Have your recent prayers been about what you want, or about what God wants?

With the definition of sin found in verse 17, sin becomes an immensely personal thing, varying from person to person. Do you think this will make us more understanding of others but harder on ourselves?

Day 326, James 5

In verses 1-6, James warns the rich, but it is the counsel in verses 7-11 regarding enduring and patience I find intriguing. Which of the following will you need to be patient with tomorrow: the Lord, a family member, others, or yourself?

Carefully read verses 13-18. They are the best in all of scripture in talking about blessing the sick and the power of prayer. What did you think of the promise about receiving a forgiveness of your sins in verse 15? If while reading these verses you feel a desire to have a blessing, please ask for one.

Blessings are one way to receive a forgiveness of sins, look for another promised in verses 19-20.

I love the book of James. What verse, or teaching from James helped you in the last five days to better live the Gospel of Jesus Christ?

Day 327, 1 Peter 1

By the time of this epistle, Peter has been the president of the Church for a couple of decades. He has seen a good amount of persecution, but in this letter, he warns of future hardships which will prove prophetic with the horrific persecutions of Nero just years away.

The prophet Joseph Smith said, "Peter penned the most sublime language of any of the apostles" (Teachings of the Prophet Joseph Smith, 301). As you read this chapter, I invite you to look not only for "sublime language," but also for sublime ideas, truths, promises, warnings, prophecies, and testimony.

What sublime things did you discover?

Day 328, 1 Peter 2

People love to collect things, and so does God. The thing that he treasures most is His children. He even calls us a "peculiar people" (:9). In Hebrew, this term is "am segulla" which means "a valued property" or "special treasure." In Greek segulla is translated as "jewels." Nothing is more important to God than His children becoming what they are meant to be.

As you read this section, look for the principles that Peter teaches about how to be and become peculiar people.

How will you be a little more peculiar today?

Day 329, 1 Peter 3

In this chapter, Peter gives several bits of counsel to different groups. In verses 1-2 he gives counsel to women who are married to men who don't believe or don't attend. In verses 3-6 he gives counsel to women about what they should and should not adorn/clothe themselves with. In verse 8 he counsels husbands. Then in verses 9-17 he gives counsel to the members of the church. There is great counsel in each of these sections, but what did Peter say that you also can testify of? If you can't answer that question, then you will need to read verse 15 again.

113

The whole reason Christ suffered was so he could bring us all before God, even the unrepentant and disobedient (:18-20). The only choice we will have in the matter will be the condition of our conscience as we stand before God (:21-22). So, because of Christ, can you stand with confidence before God the Father?

Day 330, 1 Peter 4

Peter counsels us to "arm ourselves likewise with the same mind" as Christ (:1). When we do that, we will give up our former sins and life (:2-4). We will also want the gospel to be preached to everyone, including the dead, so that they also might "live according to God in the spirit" (:6). Will you try to think more like Christ today?

Verses 7-11 are some examples of how possessing the mind of Christ will cause us to act differently. To "speak as the oracles of God" is to speak by inspiration, and not simply of yourself.

We shouldn't be surprised that life is hard and full of trials (:12-18). Nearly every scripture story is about people of faith facing a trial/hardship and prevailing with the help of God. We can trust our faithful creator to help us through all things. What is the difference between "committing the keeping of [our] souls to him in well doing" (:19), and simply enduring a trial or hardship?

Day 331, 1 Peter 5

In the final chapter of 1st Peter, he gives some counsel to specific groups like Paul did. In verses 1-4 Peter instructs the elders/leaders of the Church. Verses 5-11 contain the direction to the youth.

Pick your favorite verse of counsel to each group and then rewrite it in your own words to help you solidify the principle in your own mind.

Day 332, 2 Peter 1

People sometimes like to complicate the doctrine of having your calling and election made sure. It is simply this: when a person converts and joins Christ's Church, they are called or elected to become like Christ. That calling and election is made sure when they have or will become like Christ (:1-10). Verses 5-7 contain the necessary attributes that are required for those seeking to be "partakers of the divine nature" (:4). Which Christ like attribute are you good at and which one needs some prayerful attention?

In verses 11-15 Peter acknowledges that he will soon die.

In verses 16-21 Peter tells us exactly how he did not get a testimony and how he did. This is also instructions to us about receiving and not receiving a testimony.

Day 333, 2 Peter 2

In 1 Peter, the saints were warned about the external forces and persecution that would try to destroy the Church, but now Peter warns the saints of internal forces that are in some cases more damaging. In verses 1-9, notice what is said about false teachers and their fate. What have you learned about how to detect the false teachers from the true ones?

Speaking of those who proclaim sainthood while being unrepentant, Peter offers a barrage of phrases and words to describe them in verses 10-22. You may want to mark them. Which one do you want to make sure can never be said of you?

Day 334, 2 Peter 3

One of the major reasons that Peter wrote this epistle was to warn us about the "scoffers" in the last days that would mock and doubt the reality of the second coming of Christ (:1-4). There certainly are such scoffers. Look for what Peter says such scoffers misunderstand in verses 5-9.

In verses 10-18, Peter counters the sayings of the scoffers with his own powerful witness and warning about the second coming of Christ. What does Peter say about the second coming, and what counsel does he give regarding what we should be doing?

Day 335, 1 John 1

This letter was written to the saints in general rather than a particular group, because of widespread apostasy caused by the teachings of a particular philosophy that was gaining popularity at the time. Docetism was part of a larger movement known as Gnosticism. They believed that the spirit was good, but the body and anything to do with the body was bad. Thus, they rejected the idea that Jesus was actually born and did not experience the actual physical limitations of mortality, he only seemed to do these things. Docetism comes from the Greek dokeo, meaning "to seem" or "to appear."

With that in mind, notice how the testimony in verses 1-3 is incredibly physical. Prophets, seers, and revelators today bear this same witness if you listen closely. What do verses 3-4 say is the advantage of following those who know His voice and know His face?

I love and adore how simple and clean the truths are in verses 5-10: light, dark, sin, confession, forgiveness, and cleanse.

We sometimes talk about grey rather than light and dark. A friend pointed out to me that it is easier to see the grey and shadows when you are standing in the dark.

Day 336, 1 John 2

The last chapter was spent making sure we all knew that we were sinners. This chapter tells us that it is written to help us not sin and then declares that we have an advocate and a propitiation for our sins (:1-2, 2a, see also D&C 45:3-5). Why do these verses mean a lot or a little to you?

Lust can be a powerful feeling. Look what was said concerning the world and the lust thereof in verses 15-17. How can that knowledge give hope to those who struggle controlling those powerful feelings?

It was promised that in the last times there would be antichrists who seek to draw us away (:18-19). In verses 20-29 we are told what we must do to "abide," "remain," and "continue." I think that verse 27 is becoming increasingly more vital in the world that we live in.

Day 337, 1 John 3

What do verses 1-3 teach us about our potential as the sons and daughters of God? Do you really believe that the atonement of Jesus Christ is that powerful, that it can do what is promised in these verses?

As you read verses 4-24 ponder on each of these words: sin, righteousness, love, and commandment. When you are done take those words and craft a sentence that you believe can capture and condense the meaning of those verses.

How might verses 16-18 motivate us to do good deeds all the time and not just at Christmas?

Day 338, 1 John 4

The theme of this chapter will become apparent very quickly, the word "love" and its variations are used several times. It would be worth your time to mark each of these. As you read, consider what you believe to be the two or three most important things we learn about love in this chapter.

One of the most important questions that could be asked of each of us is "Who will you listen to?" Verses 1-6 speak about the importance to "try, test, prove, and discern" what is being presented to us in verse 1 and footnote 1b. What experiences have you had doing that?

Day 339, 1 John 5

What do verses 1-5 teach us about the causes and results from being born again?

Why might some view God's commandments as "grievous" (:3)? When, if ever, did that change for you?

Verses 7-8 contain what is called the Johannine Comma. There are words that are not found in any Greek manuscripts nor in any translation prior to the 16th century. These words are "bear record in heaven, the Father, the Word, and the Holy Ghost: and these three are one. And there are three that bear witness in the earth". These words have often caused confusion and seemed at odds with the rest of the New Testament.

I love that the JST changes the wording of verse 18 regarding those born of God to say that they "continue not in sin" instead of saying they "sinneth not" (:18b). To believe in Christ to the point that you may receive eternal life doesn't mean that you never sin, it means that at some point you stop. What difference does that little change make for you and your efforts to improve?

Day 340, 2 John

The second epistle of John has a much different feel than the other epistles. It is addressed to "the Elect Lady" (:1). It is unsure if this is a specific lady or a term to describe the Church. Some scholars have even suggested that this lady may be John's wife. This term of endearment was also used in the last days when the Lord addressed Emma Smith (D&C 25:1). It is helpful to discover more principles by viewing this letter both as a personal correspondence and as a general epistle.

In the midst of deceivers and antichrists (:7) John encourages us to "look to yourselves." We are each responsible to make sure that we don't lose our "full reward."

What does verse 10 teach you about protecting your home?

Day 341, 3 John

Here we a have a tiny personal letter of communication from John to Gaius, and yet it is included into the canon of holy scripture. Anciently, any scrap of apostolic writing was sought for and treasured. Today in the age of a plethora of prophetic writing, we may be more tempted to overlook, and under read the words of modern Apostles. How have you avoided becoming illiterate with the words of the current Prophets, seers, and revelators?

Look for what caused the greatest joy to John in verse 4. Have you had such joy? Did you bring such joy? What are you trying to do that will insure that you will have such joy?

In verses 9-11, John speaks of a situation in which a local leader is critical of the Apostles and rejects them. It must always be remembered that some of the loudest voices, come from the great and spacious building with their jeering comments and critics, are members of the House of Israel. These are members of the Church who fight against the Apostles of the The Lamb (1 Nephi 11:34-35).

Day 342, Jude

Jude is the brother of James and another half-brother of Jesus Christ (:1, Matthew 13:55, Mark 6:3). He wrote to the members of the Church. His purpose in writing had to shift from speaking about "common salvation," or the availability of salvation for everyone to instead contending for the faith that was delivered to them (:3). To contend, one must do more than just defend something, one must also promote something. When we are asked hard and challenging questions it is often an opportunity, and almost an invitation, to teach and clarify.

118

Apostasy in the New Testament has now moved from being a prophecy to a reality. Look for what Jude teaches concerning those who have lead such apostasies in the past and now in the present. What was your favorite line?

In verses 20-25, Jude gives counsel to provide protection in times of inner Church apostasy.

Elder Richard G. Scott once gave an entire Stake Conference talk just on verse 22. Why do you think this is such a great single sentence sermon?

Day 343, Revelation 1

For some additional background and information, read "Revelation of John" in the *Bible Dictionary*. What do the first two paragraphs teach you about the major theme, the name Apocalypse, and who else has seen this same vision?

This first chapter is an incredible revelation about the glorified Christ. As you read, look for everything that it tells you about him.

The book of Revelation is often viewed as frustrating because of the symbolism, but there are keys to understanding all over the scriptures. The seven stars and candlestick are explained by verse 20. The right hand is symbolic of covenant. In verse 16, the Lord doesn't have a sword coming out of this mouth, his words are like a double edged sword with power to protect or to destroy (see Hebrews 4:12).

Day 344, Revelation 2
John addresses four of the seven churches in Asia. Look for what warnings and counsel is given to each. Verses 1-7 are to Ephesus, verses 8-11 to Smyrna, verses 12-17 to Pergamos, and verses 18-29 are for Thyatira.

One of the major themes in the book of Revelation is that of overcoming. Look for what promises are made to those who overcome the world through Christ in verses 7, 11, 17, and 26-28. There is also a great cross reference to verse 17 in D&C 130:10-11.

What warnings or counsel do you think John would give to your ward, family, or to you individually to help you overcome?

Day 345, Revelation 3

Watch for the praise and counsel that John continues to give to the remaining three churches. Verses 1-7 are to Sardis, verses 8-13 to Philadelphia, and verses 14-22 to Laodicea.

In this chapter, the theme of overcoming continues. Look for how the blessings promised for overcoming are actually the promise of exaltation (:5, 12, 21).

Speaking to two different groups, John uses two different analogies about Christ and doors (:7, 20). What do you think are the lessons we should learn from each of them, because at first they appear contradictory?

Verses 15-16 teach us that the temperature of our discipleship matters. What will be your temperature today?

Day 346, Revelation 4

Chapters 1-3 dealt with John's counsel to the seven churches in Asia. Chapters 4-22 contain the apocalyptic vision of the earth's history and future. In verse 1, John is invited to come up into Heaven. From this point on, symbolism and time will shift often. John wrote in this way to both reveal and conceal the truth, just as Jesus did in the parables.

In this chapter, John is shown the celestial kingdom and all creatures worshiping God. Notice how John, like all prophets, struggled to find words to describe his experience seeing God in His glory.

If you were to try to draw what John saw you might have some trouble understanding it. Luckily there are many insights and helps that came from the prophet Joseph Smith. See footnotes 4a, 4c, 5a, 6b, and 6c. In other words, John sees a vision of God on His throne surrounded by His children and creations which He has exalted and given His understanding, power, and agency, for which they praise Him.

Day 347, Revelation 5

In chapter 5, we are shown the great premortal council were Jesus is selected as the Savior. Heavenly Father sits on His throne with His great plan written on a scroll with seven seals (:5b). Those who are watching are saddened because there is none who is worthy to act as Savior and bring Father's plan into action (:1-4). Why do you think they were so sad?

Then in verses 5-7, we are told about one who is worthy to open the book. The slain lamb is a symbol of Christ. Even before he was born and performed the atonement, people could be saved by it because it was retroactive. The number seven is symbolic of perfection and twelve is symbolic of authority and organization. Christ has that many horns because it is symbolic of His perfect power that comes from His authority. He had that many eyes because it symbolizes his perfect knowledge. Notice also that Christ takes the plan of God from His right hand or that Christ made a covenant with the Father to fulfill the plan.

How do you think you would feel if you were to have witnessed this scene? Notice how everyone else responds in verses 8-14. These verses help us better understand Job 38:4-7. What do these verses teach us to understand about who we are to worship: Heavenly Father, Jesus, or both?

Day 348, Revelation 6

In this chapter, we see the history of the earth presented through horses and colors. Horses are a symbol of conquering, so in the first seal we see a white horse or that righteousness conquers (:1-2). This is the time of Adam and Enoch. In the second seal we that sin and bloodshed prevail (:3-4). This is the time of great wickedness in the days of Noah. In the third seal we find death and famine conquering (:5-6). This is the time of Abraham, Isaac, Jacob, and Joseph. In the fourth seal we see a pale or sickly green horse of corrupt empires reigning (:7-8). This is the time of the great empires of Assyria, Babylon, Persian, Greek, and Rome. In the fifth seal we see the result of the apostasy with a vision of all of the martyrs who were slain for the truth's sake (:9-11). In the sixth seal we see many signs at the end that are meant to help prepare us for the return of Christ (:12-14). There is also a group of seven different kinds of men and people who are seeking caves and protection to abide the Savior's coming, rather than seeking Him (:15-16).

What thoughts have you had as you reviewed the history of the Bible in just a few verses?

What do you think makes the difference between people seeking for the Savior rather than hiding from him?

121

The great question of verse 17 is to be answered in chapter 7.

Day 349, Revelation 7

Verses 1-4 are interpreted in D&C 77:8-11. The 144,000 is not the number of everyone saved, that amount is found in verse (:9). Twelve is a number that represents priesthood power and organization. Multiples of twelve show an increase of priesthood fullness, power, and commitment. If you have 12,000 from each of the twelve tribes then it shows a complete priesthood and ordinances. D&C 77:11 is very helpful in understanding this.

In chapter 6, we saw that people who were rulers, rich, mighty, bond, and free were hiding from the Lamb for fear that they could not stand before Him. God has sent forth Angels, priesthood ordinances, and priesthood representatives to prepare people for the Savior. What do we learn from verses 13-17 about what made it possible for those clothed in white to be able to stand before the Lamb?

What does the promise that "God shall wipe away all tears from their eyes" mean to you (:17)?

Day 350, Revelation 8

We have no idea what is meant by "silence in heaven about the space of half an hour."

In order to understand this chapter, we will require some help from D&C 77:12-13, this may require a few readings. One of the things we learn in these verses, is that the Lord is trying to sanctify the earth for his coming. How does destruction and disaster help to sanctify the earth or the Lord's people? After a local flood, I had a friend of mine that told me how the destruction gave him and others the opportunity to do good and offer service, and by this they were able to become a little more sanctified through Christ like service. He then said, "maybe the purpose of the destruction that precedes the second coming is to change us by giving us opportunities to help."

In verses 7-12, the term "third part" is used a lot to describe the amount of destruction. The term "third part" is different than saying "one third."

122

When the term "third part" is used it doesn't mean 33.3 percent, it means not everything. God is using his power to limit the destruction and disasters.

Day 351, Revelation 9

The fallen star in verse 1 is Satan who does what he always does, seeks to blind the world by filling it with smoke, the mist of darkness, and lies by evil men who seek to plague the world as if by locust (:2-3). Notice that ultimately they can do nothing eternally bad to the Saints of God, or to other things because they are limited in what they can destroy (:4).

Most interpretations of verses 5-9, and 17-19 believe that John is describing modern warfare. What do you think?

Both of the names mentioned in verse 11 mean "destruction." Why do you think that an appropriate name for Satan? In this last battle of Armageddon 200,000,000 soldiers will fight (16). We do not know if that number is literal or symbolic.

In verses 20-21, we get a list of prominent sins in the last days and learn that the prevailing attitude is unrepentant. What small thing will you repent of today to prevent any larger issues from arising?

Day 352, Revelation 10

Since chapter 9 dealt with the fifth and sixth trumpets, it may be expected that chapter 10 would deal with the seventh. Instead we get another "mighty angel" who came down to teach John about his role in the latter-days (:1). Read verses 8-10 and look for what John had to do. Then look up D&C 77:14 to find out what it meant.

The way the book tasted is how John's mission would be. Remember that John is a translated being who will be teaching until the Savior's second coming (John 21:20-23, D&C 7). What would be sweet and bitter about teaching the gospel for that long?

The term "Elias" frequently causes confusion, like in D&C 77:14. Look up "Elias" in the *Bible Dictionary* to discover the four different uses for this term.

Day 353, Revelation 11

Let's talk about two prophets. Learn everything you can about them from verses 3-13, and D&C 77:15. What did you learn, and what questions do you have?

These events appear to be some of the last, just before the second coming. The earthquake mentioned in verse 13 is connected to D&C 45:48-53, which helps us better understand the context for verses 14-19.

The number seven in the scriptures is symbolic of perfection, or completion. The number three and a half is symbolic of something not being completed, interrupted, or arrested in its normal process. This could be the meaning of the 42nd month or three and a half year ministry of our two prophets. Their work was interrupted, likewise after three and one half day the victory of those who are celebrating the death of the two prophets will be interrupted by their being resurrected.

How does this chapter teach in several ways that God, Christ, and their witness have greater power than those who oppose them? In what ways is that power working for you in your life?

Day 354, Revelation 12

In verses 1-6, there are several symbols that can be helpful to our understanding. The women = the Church, the crown of twelve stars = the apostles, the dragon = Satan, the man child = Christ. These verses deal with the coming apostasy.

In verses 7-11, we are taken back to the war in heaven. As you read, notice how Satan tried to destroy the saints and how he was "overcome" by the saints. Remember that overcoming is one of the major themes of the book of Revelation. What has Satan "accused" you of this week? How can we use the atonement of Christ to remind us that these accusations of Satan will not stick?

Notice how Satan responds to the woman and her seed after his forced exodus from heaven, and how successful he was in verses 12-17.

Day 355, Revelation 13

We don't know much about this chapter, but many have tried, especially with the number 666. Gematria is a system where letters are assigned a number, so that numbers can mean different things or even represent people. I think the best way to view the number 666 is that it shows a deficiency and incompleteness of the number seven, which means perfection.

Instead of trying to figure what everything may mean, look closely at the characteristics of the beast and you will learn some interesting things.

Day 356, Revelation 14

The forehead is a symbolic part of the body to represent what their thoughts dwell on, their loves, and desires. Consider what that teaches us about those who follow the beast in chapter 13.

As you read, look for the difference between those who accept the gospel and what those who fight against it can expect. What did you learn about "rest" (:11-13)?

Why do you think it was important to have the gospel restored (:6) before judgement and wrath were poured out (:7-11, 17-20)?

Notice that there are two different kinds of gathering/reaping in verses 14-16 and 17-20. What is the difference and purpose of each?

Day 357, Revelation 15

In chapter 14, we learned that there would be two gatherings in the last days. The first in verses 14-16 is the gathering of the righteous. Chapter 15 describes what the righteous will experience.

For a greater understanding of what the "sea of glass mingled with fire" is, see D&C 130:1-11, or footnote 2a.

In verse 2, what did the righteous have to be victorious over to inherit this sea of glass?

Verses 6-8 describe the preparation for the gathering of the wicked.

Day 358, Revelations 16

In today's chapter we will find seven Angels who will pour out seven vials containing seven plagues upon the earth to gather the righteous and the wicked. The repetition of the number seven may be symbolically suggesting that God's judgment will be complete and perfect. How do verses 7, and 9 help you understand why the plagues continue, and don't stop?

One of the most common reasons for the destruction of people in the scriptures is when they take the lives of prophets and saints (:6, see also 3 Nephi 9:5-11, 3 Nephi 10:12, Alma 37:30, D&C 136:36).

Verse 15 contains counsel about how not to be caught unaware of these plagues. What do you think it means by "keepeth his garments?" How are you at that?

For a little more understanding about "Armageddon" look it up in the *Bible Dictionary* or the *Guide to the Scriptures.*

Day 359, Revelation 17

In the scriptures, it is common for the Church to be referred to as the bride of Christ. Just as Christ has his bride, so Satan has his. Babylon has become the term that symbolically signifies wickedness. This is not any particular church, or group, but a combination of philosophies, ideas, and corrupt beliefs. How is this bride of Satan described in verses 1-6, in terms of her character and desires?

In verses 8-12, and 15-17, look for what it says about how temporary and short Babylon's power is.

In this chapter we see all the pomp and prestige of Babylon to gather people to it and to fight against the Lamb and his bride. Look for what the result is in verse 14.

Day 360, Revelation 18

In chapter 18, we will see the promised destruction of spiritual Babylon. As you read, notice the description of Babylon and also who weeps for her when she falls. Why are they weeping, and what is it that they will miss? Why do you think we have such a hard time bidding Babylon farewell?

Look for how quickly the destruction of Babylon comes in verses 8, 10, 17, and 19.

What additional insights can we learn about the destruction of Babylon from verses 20, 24 and 1 Nephi 11:35-36?

Day 361, Revelation 19

Since Revelation 8, we have been preparing for the second coming of Jesus Christ, the great and terrible day of the Lord. For the righteous, the second coming is a great day (:1-6). It is also called the "the marriage supper of the Lord" (:9). What did the righteous do to be ready for this supper according to verses 7-10?

Verses 11-16 is a description of Christ at his coming. Look at the cross references in footnote 13a to discover why the Savior will be wearing red at his coming.

In verses 17-21, we learn that the second coming will be terrible for the wicked. "The supper of the great God" in verse 17 differs from the "marriage supper of the Lamb" (:9). The supper of the great God is for the beasts and fowls to feed upon the bodies of those slain in the battle of Armageddon. There are two suppers, which one are you preparing for? How are you preparing?

Day 362, Revelation 20

Verses 1-6 describe the events during the Savior's thousand year reign on the earth, or the millennium. For an interesting detail about how Satan is bound, see 1 Nephi 22:26. After looking at that reference, is there any reason that Satan and his influence cannot be bound in your life right now?

In verses 7-10, we learn that there will be a battle at the end of the millennium between Satan and his followers versus the saints called the battle of Gog and Magog. Notice how they are defeated and their destination. For additional information check out D&C 29:22; D&C 43:31; and D&C 88:110-116. Why do you think it is important to know that Satan never has any lasting power?

What great things can you learn about judgment and resurrection from verses 11-15?

Day 363, Revelation 21

At the end of the Millennium the earth will undergo a second transformation. This time it will change from a Terrestrial kingdom into a Celestial kingdom. See what you can learn about the Celestial kingdom from this chapter.

Why do you think it is important for us to know the end result of the Atonement mentioned in verse 4?

According to verse 22, why will temples not be needed in the Celestial kingdom?

The promise for overcoming Satan and this world is an inheritance of "all things" (:7). This is more about the attributes of God than about his stuff. What qualities do our Heavenly parents possess that you would one day like to have?

Day 364, Revelation 22

The chapter heading indicates that we will continue to learn about the "splendor" of the Celestial kingdom. As you read verses 1-5, what do you think is splendid?

What do verses 8-9 teach you about worship? By the way, this is the second time that John has experienced this lesson (Revelation 19:10).

As you read verses 10-20, ponder on the importance of the words "let," "may," and "come."

Verses 18-19 are often misused to discredit the book that we will study next year, but a simple understanding of when the book of Revelation was written compared with other New Testament books, knowledge of the word "Bible" (see Bible Dictionary "Bible" 1-2 paragraphs), and awareness of Deuteronomy 4:2 can clear this up.

Thank you for studying with us this year. We invite you to continue as we

128

study the Book of Mormon next year, and wish with John the grace of the Lord Jesus Christ to be with you.

Day, 365

What will you study today?

Bibliography

Ballard, Melvin J. (1949) "The Sacramental Covenant" Delivered at a June Conference; printed in Bryant S. Hinckley, *Sermons and Missionary Services of Melvin Joseph Ballard*. Salt Lake City: Deseret Book.

Bednar, David. A. (2014) To Sweep the Earth as with a Flood. *Campus Education Week at Brigham Young University in Provo, Utah*.

Benson, Ezra. Taft. (1989) A Mighty Change of Heart. *Ensign*, Oct. Salt Lake City: The Church of Jesus Christ of Latter-day Saints.

Gaskill, Alonzo. L. (2003) *The Lost Language of Symbolism An Essential Guide For Recognizing And Interpreting Symbols of The Gospel*. Salt Lake City: Deseret Book.

Hanks, Marion D. (1974) Forgiveness: The Ultimate Form of Love. Ensign. Jan. Salt Lake City: The Church of Jesus Christ of Latter-day Saints.

Hinckley, Gordon B. (1976) An Honest Man – God's Noblest Work. *Ensign*, May. Salt Lake City: The Church of Jesus Christ of Latter-day Saints.

Holland, Jeffery. R. (2012) The First Great Commandment. *Ensign*, Nov. Salt Lake City: The Church of Jesus Christ of Latter-day Saints.

Holland, Jeffery. R. (2010) The Best Is Yet To Be. *Ensign*, Jan. Salt Lake City: The Church of Jesus Christ of Latter-day Saints.

Holland, Jeffrey. R. (2007) The Tongues of Angels. *Ensign*, May. Salt Lake City: The Church of Jesus Christ of Latter-day Saints.

Holland, Jeffery. R. (1999) An High Priest of Good Things to Come. *Ensign*, Nov. Salt Lake City: The Church of Jesus Christ of Latter-day Saints.

Holland, Jeffery. R. (1999) The Hands of the Fathers. *Ensign*, May. Salt Lake City: The Church of Jesus Christ of Latter-day Saints.

McConkie, Bruce. R. (1971a) *Doctrinal New Testament Commentary Volume II Acts-Philippians*. Salt Lake City: Bookcraft.

McConkie, Bruce. R. (1971b) *Doctrinal New Testament Commentary Volume III Colossians-Revelation*. Salt Lake City: Bookcraft.

McKay, David. O. (1911) *Conference Report*, Oct. Salt Lake City: The Church of Jesus Christ of Latter-day Saints.

Monson, Thomas. S. (1986)A Provident Plan-A Precious Promise. *Ensign*, April. Salt Lake City: The Church of Jesus Christ of Latter-day Saints.

Ogden, K.D., & Skinner, A.C. (1998) *New Testament Apostles Testify of Christ A Guide For Acts Through Revelation*. Salt Lake City: Deseret Book.

Palmer, S.J., Keller, R.R., Choi, D.S., & Toronto J.A. (1997) *Religions of The World A Latter-day Saint View*. Prove: Brigham Young University.

Smith. Joseph. Jr. (1976) Teachings of the Prophet Joseph Smith. Salt Lake City, Utah: *Desert Book*.

Talmage, James. E. (1981) *Jesus The Christ*. Salt Lake City: The Church of Jesus Christ of Latter-day Saints.

Wirthlin, Joseph. B. (1993) Our Lord and Savior. Ensign, Nov. Salt Lake City: The Church of Jesus Christ of Latter-day Saints.

Made in the USA
San Bernardino, CA
18 September 2018